Sentence Combining

A Composing Book

This book is printed on acid-free paper.

SENTENCE COMBINING
A Composing Book

Credits appear on page 235 and on this page by reference.

9 0 DOC DOC   0

ISBN 0-07-062535-2

This book was set in Goudy Old Style by Better Graphics, Inc.
The editors were Alison Husting Zetterquist, Laurie PiSierra, and Jean Akers;
the designer and illustrator was Armen Kojoyian;
the production supervisor was Annette Mayeski.
R. R. Donnelley & Sons Company was printer and binder.

Library of Congress Cataloging-in-Publication Data

Strong, William, (date).
    Sentence combining: a composing book / William Strong. —3rd ed.
        p.   cm.
    ISBN 0-07-062535-2
    1. English language—Rhetoric.   2. English language—Grammar.
    I. Title.
    [PE1408.S7713   1994]
    808'.042—dc20   93-20825

For
My Folks
Whose Words Still Whisper
in My Inner Ear
and Here

CONTENTS

UNIT 2

Intermediate Combining 55

UNIT 3
Advanced Combining   99

UNIT 4

Unclustered Combining 139

UNIT 5

Recombining Practice 173

APPENDIX A

Sentence Combining and Writing Process 209

APPENDIX B

Sentence and Paragraph Strategies 221

PREFACE

The third edition of *Sentence Combining: A Composing Book* continues to emphasize playful but thoughtful practice in sentence construction, drawing on research in language learning and writing. Exercises in combining and revising remain at the heart of the book, just as opportunities for collaborative learning remain central to its teaching approaches.

Here, three sections of "open" combining (Units 1, 2, and 3) are organized in order of increasing difficulty. Additionally, all sentence-combining (SC) exercises have been revised and updated, with material added to address the needs and interests of a diverse (and often nontraditional) audience. Unit 3 offers a new emphasis on *expository and persuasive* writing in a multiparagraph format—this to provide practice with the discourse modes so essential for college success.

Concluding the third edition are unclustered SC exercises, as well as recombining work drawn from highly skilled writers. The unclustered format (Unit 4) helps students decide "what goes with what"—basic decisions, of course, for any developing writer. Unit 5 invites students to recombine the "deconstructed" sentences of superb stylists, to study how their versions compare with original texts, and to write follow-up essays. Recombining emphasizes, in particular, authors from diverse backgrounds—among them, Amy Tan, William Least Heat Moon, Maya Angelou, and Gary Soto.

Finally, instructors familiar with earlier editions will note that this one contains new back-of-the-book lessons. Appendix A, "Sentence Combining and Writing Process," helps student writers understand the dynamics of writing and provides advice on seven strategies for generating ideas. Appendix B, "Sentence and Paragraph Strategies," provides minilessons dealing with parallel structure, sentence variety, choosing effective sentences, paragraph organization, and paragraph packaging.

Typical SC exercises feature a brief introduction, a Writing Tip, and an Invitation for follow-up writing. The Invitations serve as springboards for personal application of skills. Writings that emerge from SC Invitations may be kept in portfolios, much like journal entries, and then used for in-class workshops or for points of departure in instructor-designed assignments. Thus, while the exercises develop *syntactic fluency*—a fact well-documented in SC research literature—the follow-up Invitations develop what most instructors call *writing fluency*, an increased willingness to commit words to paper.

In-class workshops provide students with feedback on the success of their combining work, as well as encouragement for their follow-up writing. A

Sentence Combining

A Composing Book

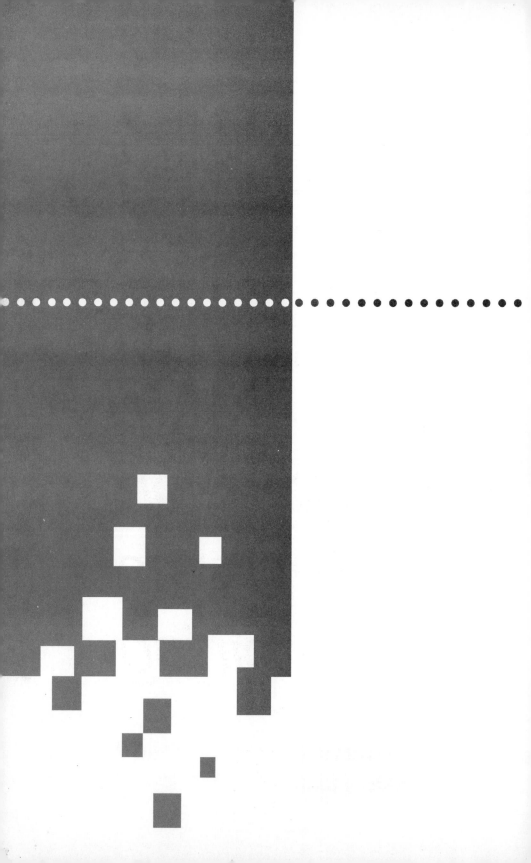

Introduction to Sentence Combining

Sentence Combining is a book with a simple aim: to help you strengthen your writing skills and understand stylistic choices in written English. Its approach invites you to put short, choppy sentences together to make ones that are interesting and readable. By doing this, you'll explore *options* in writing and move closer toward a clear, personal style.

As the subtitle says, this is a composing book. And composing means *doing* writing, not just talking about it. So let's start with an illustration:

> Sentence combining improves fluency.
>
> It transfers skills to real writing.
>
> This is according to researchers

One way to combine these sentences is probably obvious to you:

> Sentence combining improves fluency and transfers skills to real writing, according to researchers.

But you also have other options, ones you might prefer. Here are just a few choices:

> Besides improving fluency, sentence combining transfers skills to real writing, according to researchers.
> > OR
> According to researchers, sentence combining improves fluency; in addition, it transfers skills to real writing.
> > OR
> Not only does sentence combining improve fluency, according to researchers, but it also transfers skills to real writing.
> > OR
> Researchers say that improvements in fluency—and a transfer of skills to real writing—result from sentence combining.

Once you play with sentence options, you begin to break loose from the "and-and-and" style of writing you mastered in elementary school. In addition, working with options sets the stage for other choices you make as a writer—choices like wording, sequencing of ideas, and paragraph development. In short, you take charge of your writing with practice in sentence combining.

JUST DO IT

Writing skills are best learned through experience—through *doing*. And doing writing means taking chances. Clearly, no one learns to swim by sitting on the bank and playing it safe. The same is true for telling jokes, riding skateboards, programming a computer, making love, organizing the block for political action—and writing. We learn what we do.

But taking chances, especially in writing, may give you the jitters. After all, you've been taught that correctness counts, and you don't want to risk mistakes. Besides, mistakes in writing can make you look stupid and lower your grade. So you ask yourself: Mistakes? Who needs them?

You do, of course. The simple truth is that *no one learns anything, including writing, without making mistakes.* For example, in learning childhood skills—talking, walking upright, reading—you made lots of mistakes. So lighten up. Mistakes help you learn by showing you what *not* to do. No one is going to penalize you or embarrass you for the mistakes you make in sentence combining.

Of course, skills are also learned through *practice.* If you want to get better at skateboarding, playing the guitar, or creating sentences, you practice a lot, not just once in a while. Moreover, if you want to increase your physical strength and endurance—or your mental concentration and memory—you *train* with those ends in mind, gradually increasing the level of challenge. Think of sentence combining as a kind of language workout, a training program for writing.

Finally, skills are acquired through *feedback.* Beginning skiers, for example, need feedback about what's causing them to flail hopelessly out of control down the slopes. Coaching, visual imagery, videotape—all of these can help novices practice the basic moves so essential to the smooth, "natural" flow of expert skiing. And the act of skiing itself—sometimes exhilarating, sometimes exasperating—provides additional feedback.

Feedback about your skill in sentence combining comes from three human sources: your instructor, other students in class, and yourself. Sometimes your instructor will offer advice on sentence construction or point out usage principles. Often you'll team up with other students in workshops that compare various sentences, yours included. And frequently you'll be reading and rereading your own sentences, tinkering with wording and making adjustments in punctuation so that the writing *feels* right.

SENTENCE COMBINING IN ACTION

If you've flipped through the book, you've seen lists of sentences, mostly organized into clusters. Let's consider options for the cluster of sentences shown below. Try whispering the options for sentence combining (SC, for short) to hear their differences.

> The sub had faked to the baseline.
>
> The sub had twisted past his defender.
>
> The sub had banked a shot off the glass.
>
> The sub had sent the crowd into ecstasy.
>
>
>
> The sub had faked to the baseline, twisted past his defender, banked a shot off the glass, and sent the crowd into ecstasy.
>
> OR
>
> After faking to the baseline and twisting past his defender, the sub had banked a shot off the glass, sending the crowd into ecstasy.
>
> OR
>
> The sub—faking to the baseline, twisting past his defender, banking a shot off the glass—had sent the crowd into ecstasy.

Reading through these SC options, you may be surprised at their differences. All are clear and correct, yet each achieves a different effect. Which is best? That depends on *context*, the larger paragraph of which these sentences are a part. Perhaps your vote, in some contexts, would go to this sentence rather than the ones above:

> With a fake to the baseline, the sub had twisted past his defender and then banked a shot off the glass. The crowd was ecstatic.

Notice the impact of this option—a short, dramatic sentence standing by itself. This example shows that the goal of combining isn't simply to make long sentences. Rather, the goal is to make *good* sentences and to choose the *best* sentence for the situation. Sometimes you'll deliberately choose a short, simple sentence over a more complex one. Why? Because brevity packs a punch.

The point, remember, is that SC exercises have many right answers. You can rearrange sentences, change nouns like *ecstasy* into adjectives like *ecstatic,* and even add details if you choose. By working with sentences in such creative ways, you make them your own and speed up the transfer of skills to your real writing. Here's an example of rearranged sentences with added details:

> An ecstatic crowd had watched the sub fake to the baseline and twist past a frantic, backpedaling defender—his shot banking softly off the glass to send the championship into overtime.

PARAGRAPHS: A CONTEXT FOR COMBINING

In SC exercises with clustered sentences, you'll see two numbers next to each sentence: the first refers to the *cluster,* the second to the *sentence* within the cluster. Double numbers speed up in-class discussion and work in small groups.

Some activities—like the one below—have less than twenty sentences. But regardless of length, this book's exercises develop your sense of written paragraphs. Because sentences are linked together in a paragraph context, your SC practice can help you understand the structure of paragraphs—the way sentences "hang together."

⊃ *Looking Back*

1.1   Shadows filled the coach's office.
1.2   The coach bent over his metal desk.
1.3   He cleaned out the bulging files.

2.1   He was ready to dump an envelope.
2.2   A photo caught his attention.
2.3   The photo was fading.
2.4   The photo was from an earlier era.

3.1 The young man's face was thin.
3.2 The young man's face was determined.
3.3 His eyes hungered for a chance to play.

4.1 The coach thought back.
4.2 The coach remembered something.
4.3 He had pulled a sub off the bench.
4.4 He had yelled instructions.
4.5 The lad had ignored them.

5.1 The sub had faked to the baseline.
5.2 The sub had twisted past his defender.
5.3 The sub had banked a shot off the glass.
5.4 The sub had sent the crowd into ecstasy.

Each cluster represents a potential sentence in a paragraph. Of course, you're in charge of your learning. Therefore, it's you who decides whether to split a given cluster into two sentences, leave it as is, or combine it with another. In this way you can adjust the exercise so that it meets your skill level.

How do you do such an exercise? First, scan the sentences so that you sense the paragraph context; as you do this, *whisper* a possible sentence or two—nothing fancy, just the first ones that come to mind. As a second step, try *different* sentence openers or tinker with phrasing, perhaps rearranging ideas or experimenting with connectors. Then write out the sentence choices that *feel and sound right*—the ones that seem to work best in context.

Because these steps take time, you may be tempted to hurry them. Resist the temptation. After all, there's no point in stringing words and phrases in random, haphazard order. The idea is to stay in charge—and to develop your sentence skills with care. Sentence combining works when you work *with* it.

Your instructor may assign SC exercises as part of a regular homework routine, similar to keeping a journal. Or perhaps you'll combine sentences in class. Whatever the case, you'll often have one or more polished paragraphs in hand. Your instructor may collect your work for photocopying, put you in a workshop group with others, or hold a class discussion. Perhaps you'll be asked to put your paragraph on the board or copy it onto a transparency. If your school has a computer lab, your paragraphs—along with others from your class—may be projected on a large screen or monitor.

Imagine such a workshop situation, with everyone's work on the line, yours included. Find the *best* paragraph below—Version X, Y, or Z—and claim it as your own. Take your time with this reading, listening carefully to the sentences in each paragraph.

> **VERSION X.** (1) As shadows filled the coach's office, the coach bent over his metal desk and cleaned out the bulging files. (2) He was ready to dump an envelope when a photo caught his attention. (3) The photo was fading and from an earlier era. (4) The young man's face was thin and determined, and his eyes hungered for a chance to play. (5) The coach thought back and remembered something. (6) He had pulled a sub off the bench and yelled instructions, but the lad had ignored them. (7) The sub had faked to the baseline, twisted past his defender, and banked a shot off the glass. (8) The sub had sent the crowd into ecstasy.

> **VERSION Y.** (1) With shadows filling his office, the coach bent over his metal desk, cleaning out the bulging files. (2) He was ready to dump an envelope, but a fading photo from an earlier era caught his attention. (3) The young man's face was thin and determined; his eyes hungered for a chance to play. (4) As the coach thought back, he remembered that he had pulled a sub off the bench and yelled instructions that were ignored by the lad. (5) The sub had faked to the baseline and twisted past his defender. (6) His shot, banked off the glass, had sent the crowd into ecstasy.

> **VERSION Z.** (1) In a shadow-filled office, the coach bent over his metal desk to clean out bulging files. (2) He was ready to dump an envelope when a fading photo from an earlier era caught his attention. (3) The young man's face, thin and determined, hungered for a chance to play. (4) The coach thought back, remembering that he had pulled a sub off the bench and then yelled instructions that the lad ignored. (5) Faking to the baseline and twisting past his defender, the sub had banked a shot off the glass—the crowd's ticket to ecstasy.

LANGUAGE AS TEACHER

Let's pause for a moment before discussing the paragraph you've chosen as the best of the three. What do we *mean* by "best"? How do we know it when we see and hear it?

Making such a choice is both complex and personal—a little like a clothing decision. After being attracted to a specific garment, for example, you find the right size as well as the colors that complement your skin tones. Your decision is informed by magazines and TV, as well as by the fashions you see at school, on the job, or in your neighborhood. You develop a *feel* for what's socially appropriate. And because you're alert to prices, you probably know the difference between a rip-off and a bargain.

Similarly, your choice of the best paragraph depends on what sounds good and feels right to you. It's based on your own standards and values. Everything you've ever read—from comics to classics—helps you know what you like and don't like about a particular piece of writing. Put another way, written language has been teaching you its complex lessons for many years, just like an infinitely patient teacher.

Experts agree that reading skills support your skills as a writer. In fact, although you may not realize it, reading has taught you far more about spelling, punctuation, and sentence structure than any lists, drills, or grammar books you may have studied. The closer you read—and the *more* you read—the better you'll understand how writing works; and the *better* you understand writing, of course, the more informed your decisions will be.

Since language becomes your teacher whenever you read, think how much you *could* learn if you consciously attended to the writing lessons all around you. First, you'd answer all your own questions about punctuation, usage, and phrasing by simply observing what good writers do. And then— because knowledge is power—you'd apply what you had learned, making it your own.

This is exactly what we do with sentence combining. When you engage in SC practice and follow-up analysis, what you're doing is *reading like a writer.* Let's see what you can learn from paying attention to Versions X, Y, and Z, the three paragraphs from the "Looking Back" exercise above.

VERSION X.   Many readers see this paragraph as okay—but maybe the least effective of the three. All sentences, except the opener, have the same rhythm. The paragraph seems to lack variety—like a monotone speaker. Sentence 1 is awkward; it repeats the word *coach* rather than using a pronoun like *he* or *his* to smooth out the phrasing. Sentences 2 and 3 are choppy; see also sentences 7 and 8, which could be combined. A pattern of "and-and-and" runs through the sentences.

VERSION Y.   Most readers see this as an excellent paragraph. It has sentence variety and uses pronouns (*he* and *his*) in skilled ways to substitute for nouns. Sentence 1 is very well constructed; sentence 3 provides an effective contrast to the longer sentences that surround it. The sentences that follow are clear and varied. Sentence 6, in particular, makes nice use of interruption for closing emphasis. This paragraph shows skill and good control.

VERSION Z. Some readers, though not all, strongly prefer this paragraph to the other two. It uses sophisticated phrasing ("shadow-filled office") in sentence 1. The sentences that follow—especially sentence 3—show excellent control and variety. Sentences 4 and 5 work well; both use participle constructions (in the phrases that begin with "remembering" and "faking") but in different positions. Sentence 5 ends with a flourish—an interesting surprise for the reader. All in all, this paragraph has style.

Does the above analysis mean that Version X is "wrong"? Of course not. What this analysis suggests is that Version X has room for specific improvements. The alternative sentences in Versions Y and Z provide clues to what those changes might be.

The point of comparing paragraphs in this way is to develop your critical reading skills—the habit of *reading like a writer*. The focus here is not on content, because the ideas are virtually the same. Instead, SC practice directs you to the *writing itself*—and the writer's skill in relating one sentence to another.

If you have a how-to-do-it interest in writing, you can probably see the potential of this approach, one that has rewarded thousands of students just like you.

DEVELOPING SPEECH-INTO-WRITING SKILLS

Language acts as your teacher in another way too. Since birth, you've been enrolled in an intensive, nonstop language course—one called *talking*. You've learned incredibly complex patterns of syntax without any books, teaching machines, or lectures. Just by being exposed to speech and using it in everyday life, you've figured out its basic rules. You build on such knowledge when you develop writing skills because writing is "frozen speech."

Of course, there are also differences between speech and writing. In conversation, people let you know when you're not making sense, and you sometimes *use* their responses to clarify things in your own mind. In writing, by contrast, you often must *imagine* the reader's response and develop your message without the benefit of a back-and-forth interchange. Moreover, you generally never know what's really going on in your reader's mind.

Learning to write means building on the speech skills you already possess—and transforming that power into print. Again, this is *not* to say that talk and writing are exactly alike. What it means, quite simply, is that writing skills develop from (and extend) the patterns of talk that you learned as a child.

And what if English is not your first language? For you, learning written English may pose special challenges. On the other hand, you probably don't have the same "blinders" to language that some native speakers have. And because you already possess a wide array of thinking and survival skills—not to mention those of your native language—you can use these to your advantage as a learner. In vocabulary learning, for example, you can use words you already know to "hook" new words in English.

SC exercises build on your deeply internalized patterns of speech. Working with SC exercises helps you see these patterns in print; but equally important, working with others helps you learn many *new* patterns, ones not usually found in talk. As you pay attention, your speech-into-writing skills begin to develop.

In Units 1, 2, and 3—basic, intermediate, and advanced levels of "open" combining—you can pay attention by noticing the Writing Tip that follows each exercise. This feature offers specific hints about connectors, sentence openers, or other writing moves. Here's an example from the "Looking Back" exercise:

Writing Tip   Try using a participle (like *remembering* or *faking*) in clusters 4 and 5.

It's worth noting here that Unit 3 offers multiparagraph practice in *expository and persuasive writing*—the modes essential for college success. In this section, SC exercises serve much like "bookends" for your writing. Simply put, the purpose of Unit 3 is to help you with organizational skills as well as sentence skills, particularly as you read Appendix A and Appendix B.

Units 4 and 5 present new challenges. In Unit 4, for example, you practice deciding "what goes with what"—developing your skills of sequencing and arranging content. In Unit 5, you work with the sentences of skilled professional writers—comparing your combined version with the original text. This process helps extend your skills of reading like a writer. Also, Unit 5 exercises offer a variety of Invitations for personal writing.

BEYOND SENTENCE COMBINING

"Wait a minute," you may be thinking. "Combining may teach me skills, but how do I *apply* what I've learned?"

The answer to this question depends on your response to the Invitations that accompany SC exercises. As the name implies, these are optional activities, not command performances. Most invite a paragraph or two of writing to move you *beyond* combining. In this way SC provides a springboard for your writing practice. Here's an Invitation for the "Looking Back" exercise:

Invitation Extend this story by focusing on the coach or the sub in your follow-up writing. Why did the coach save this photograph? What happened to the sub?

Clearly, some Invitations will hold more appeal than others; clearly, too, no one expects you to respond to all of them. The point is simply to respond to ones that interest you and to try, consciously, to apply the writing skills you've been learning. This process of modeling and imitation has worked for others; in fact, its roots go back 2500 years in western civilization.

Here's one example of writing that might emerge from the Invitation above:

> It was in overtime, the final twenty seconds of the game, that the sub came through again. Snagging a pass, he whipped the ball across court to set up a fast break that scored an easy two points. Then he intercepted another in-bounds pass and whirled into the air with a high arching jump shot. It hit the back rim, then lifted like a rising moon against a glass horizon. Taking his own rebound, the sub cut past a weak defender and went up again—his fingers now following the ball as it left his hand. This time it dropped like a stone, hardly touching the net. A wild melee had followed as a hometown crowd swarmed to the floor, engulfing the team and the grinning substitute, whose sweaty arms embraced the coach's neck. "Hey," he had shouted. "Thanks a lot, Dad."

To develop writing fluency, many students alternate their daily practice in a writing journal with SC exercises and follow-up Invitations. Such a plan makes sense. It balances the freedom of personal journal writing with the structure and challenge of brief skill-building activities.

You'll find it valuable to keep your SC practice in a working portfolio. As you look back at your SC work over several weeks, you'll probably be pleasantly surprised by the clear improvements in quality. Also, many students use this portfolio as a starting point for their instructor's writing assignments.

Make sure to read "Sentence Combining and Writing Process" (Appendix A) and "Sentence and Paragraph Strategies" (Appendix B) at the back of this book. Appendix A, which provides tips on generating ideas, will help you understand SC practice in the context of writing process. Appendix B offers mini-lessons that deal with parallelism and sentence variety, choosing effective sentences, and concepts of paragraphing.

Good luck with *Sentence Combining!*

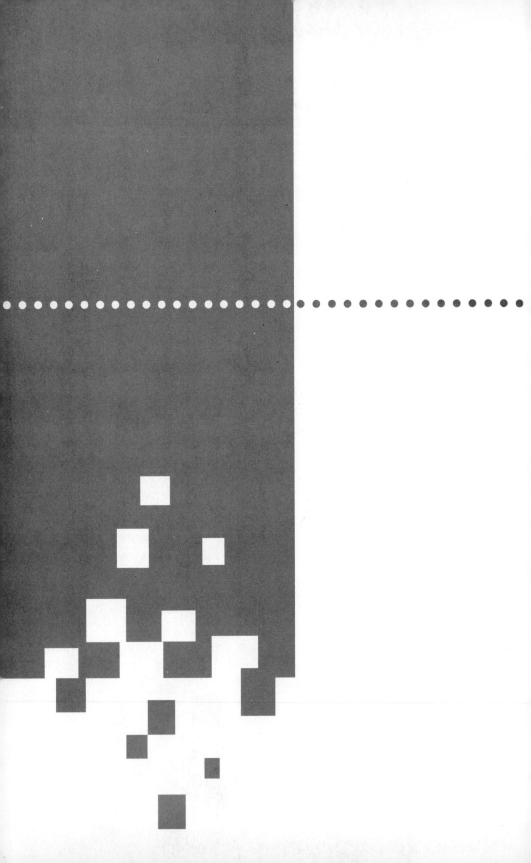

Warm-Up Combining

In the Introduction you learned how people spend childhood in an intense language course, with the world acting as their teacher. We learn to talk naturally and painlessly, without any instruction, drills, or formal study. Simply by being exposed to talk and trying to make sense, we internalize complex signaling systems of language. By age five or so, we're virtual experts in the basic speech patterns of our native tongue.

The implications of this fact are important. Practice in sentence combining doesn't teach you anything new about language. What it does instead is build upon what you've already learned. You have a wealth of language power "beneath the surface," just waiting to be tapped. Combining brings many sentence patterns to the surface so you can refine them in your writing. It also strengthens your transcribing fluency and helps you relax.

SPEECH-INTO-WRITING PRACTICE

Because speech is our primary language system, sentence combining is basically an oral process. It invites you to do what skilled writers do— namely, to whisper sentences to yourself and to select those that *sound* best. It develops your skill of listening for the swaying, elegant curves of some sentences and the hard, rhythmic regular punch of others. It helps you craft your prose so that pause—and emphasis—can do their work.

Although writing *depends* on speech, it also goes *beyond* it. You can prove this to yourself by transcribing a few minutes of tape-recorded talk from school (a lecture in your history course, say) and reading it back to yourself. You'll find that the recorded sentences don't really sound like the ones from magazines or books. The alternate test, of course, is to read writing aloud. Do the sentences on this page, for example, sound like talk?

In speech, the process of combining (or transforming) ideas is completely automatic, and we're not usually aware of our own processes. In writing, however, the process often causes us to pause. Why? Because writing is one-word-after-another-in-space. The spoken sentence, once uttered, is gone forever; the written sentence, on the other hand, can be studied, tinkered with, turned over and over. Its options multiply before our eyes. We imagine different possibilities because we *see* the sentence before us.

In sentence combining, then, you'll focus on synthesis—how sentences go together—rather than on grammatical analysis. Our underlying assumption is that complex sentences are comprised of smaller ones (called "kernel sentences" by linguists). You'll learn a variety of ways to connect and relate ideas so then you train an automatic pilot for sentence construction.

Having an automatic pilot frees your mind to think about the important issues of writing—content, organization, and audience. Our aim in such training isn't to name parts of speech or recite rules; instead, we're trying to explore sentence options. You'll probably write longer sentences with increased modification; but you'll learn how to tighten your writing too.

As a natural outgrowth of your work with sentence options, you're bound to increase your working knowledge of punctuation and grammar. Of course, a technical knowledge of grammar—without application—will not improve your ability to make sentences with grace and precision any more than a knowledge of chemistry—without application—will make you a gourmet chef. Grammar and punctuation are tools of the trade, nothing more. While such tools are useful, your skill as a writer depends mainly on your ability to *make* sentences, not on your ability to label them.

Hints on Sentence Combining

When doing SC exercises on your own or with others, remember that your goal is *good* sentences—the best you can muster—not simply long ones. Leaving a sentence uncombined is always one of your basic choices. Why? Because brevity is often better.

It's also worth remembering that you learn nothing by putting words together in random or haphazard ways. Take your time. The idea, after all, is to take control—and to improve your skills by *paying attention* to the choices you make.

Here are some hints on working with exercises:

1. As you combine sentences, *listen* to them. Say them aloud to a writing partner, or whisper them to yourself. Take risks by experimenting with new patterns. Imitate sentences that appeal to you.
2. To activate decision making, jot down a sentence. Then read it in the context of previous sentence choices. Make revisions as necessary. When you decide which version you prefer, try to figure out why.
3. Compare your sentences with those of other students. Watch for stylistic patterns—habits of writing—in your sentences. Consciously *vary* your patterns to flex your language muscles.
4. Use the Writing Tip feature regularly. Then, as you finish an SC exercise, double-check your punctuation and spelling for accuracy. Make proofreading a regular habit, a matter of personal pride.

5.   Go *beyond* the exercises by accepting Invitations for follow-up writing. Share this writing with workshop partners, and enjoy what they have written. As you look over this writing, find opportunities to *apply* SC skills.

Don't draw the conclusion from these hints that SC practice is grim business. Sentence combining is fun because the process has lots of right answers and because it allows you to learn from others, not just from confusing rules.

So think of it as a game you can't lose.

And play for all you're worth.

⊃ *Bungee Jumping*

"It's a rush," some people claim—strapping bungee cords to their ankles and leaping out into space. Would you do it on a dare?

1.1   The moment of truth arrived.
1.2   Max had felt raw panic.

2.1   He stood atop the bungee tower.
2.2   He felt a jackhammer in his chest.

3.1   His mind screamed one repeated thought.
3.2   "What am I doing here?"

4.1   Far below was the parking lot.
4.2   Car windows glinted in the sun.

5.1   Traffic streamed by on the highway.
5.2   A small plane droned in the distance.

6.1   Max squeezed his eyes shut.
6.2   Max wished he'd never accepted the dare.

7.1   "You're eighteen," he told himself.
7.2   "You're going to die," he told himself.

8.1 Then suddenly he was weightless.
8.2 He was falling headlong toward earth.

Writing Tip Try adding an *-ing* ending to one of the verbs in cluster 2. Try *where* as a connector in cluster 4.

Invitation Give your reasons why Max and thousands of other Americans have "taken the plunge" with bungee jumping. Explain why you will (or won't) follow his lead.

⊃ Value Judgment

Cheating in schools is a common problem—one that forces value judgments. What do you think? Is cheating on exams okay?

1.1 Carol was working hard on her test.
1.2 Sue slipped her a note.

2.1 She unfolded the paper carefully.
2.2 She didn't want her teacher to see.

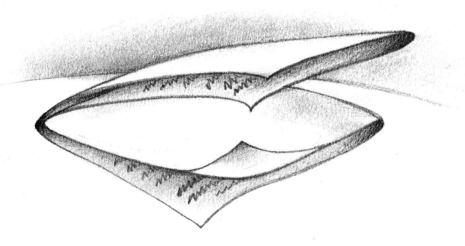

3.1 The note asked for help on a question.
3.2 The question was important.

4.1 Carol looked down at her paper.
4.2 She thought about the class's honor system.

5.1 Everyone had made a pledge.
5.2 The pledge was not to cheat.

6.1 Carol didn't want to go back on her word.
6.2 Sue was her best friend.

7.1 Time was running out.
7.2 She had to make up her mind.

8.1 Her mouth felt dry.
8.2 Her mouth felt tight.

Writing Tip In cluster 6, try a connector like *but, although,* or *however.* Note that a connector like *because* does not make sense.

Invitation Finish the story by explaining what Carol does and the reasons for her value judgment. Or write about a personal value judgment that you had to make.

⊃ Street-Smart

Does loud rap music turn you on? How about boom boxes? Stewart thinks everybody shares his tastes—and maybe two observers do.

1.1 Stewart swaggered down the street.
1.2 He clicked his fingers.
1.3 He popped his fingers.

2.1 He was tuned into pulsing rhythms.
2.2 The rhythms came from his boom box.

3.1 The sound jerked ahead of him.
3.2 The sound bounced ahead of him.
3.3 The sound was hard-core rap music.

4.1 It announced his arrival to shoppers.
4.2 It announced his arrival to storekeepers.
4.3 It announced his arrival to girls in the café.

5.1 One girl giggled and blushed.
5.2 She tried to look bored.
5.3 She tried to look very cool.

6.1 Another arched one eyebrow.
6.2 She covered her mouth with one hand.
6.3 Her mouth was smiling.

7.1 Stewart circled around both of them.
7.2 Stewart did his lip-synch routine.
7.3 Stewart let his shoulders dip and bob.

8.1 He enjoyed the street scene's tension.
8.2 He enjoyed their flirtation.
8.3 Their flirtation was coy.

Writing Tip   Try combining clusters 3 and 4 by using *announcing* as a key word.

Invitation   Describe what happens next in this street scene. Or describe an incident from the street scene you see every day.

⊃ *Cruising Main*

Why is cruising such a popular activity for many young adults? Think about one experience, and share it with workshop partners.

1.1 The night is warm and bright.
1.2 Low riders cruise the main drag.
1.3 The low riders are glittering.

2.1 Their bodies scream for attention.
2.2 Their bodies are sleek.
2.3 Their bodies are gleaming.

> He had work hard and had gotton a Raise that was Unexpected.

3.1 There is a rumble of exhaust.
3.2 The rumble is thundering.
3.3 The cars pause at stoplights.
3.4 Drivers rev their engines.

4.1 Lights explode off the scene.
4.2 The explosion is soft.
4.3 The scene is shimmering.

5.1 The boys wear their masks.
5.2 The masks are sullen.
5.3 The masks are tough-looking.

6.1 The girls are decked out in hairdos.
6.2 The hairdos are bizarre.
6.3 The hairdos are just for cruising.

7.1 It is like a supercarnival.
7.2 The supercarnival is weird.
7.3 It is part of our mating rites.
7.4 The mating rites are national.

8.1 This happens at the far end of Main Street.
8.2 The cars circle through a parking lot.
8.3 The parking lot is deserted.
8.4 The cars head back the other way.

Writing Tip Try opening cluster 7 with the word *like* for sentence variety.

Invitation Use this paragraph to introduce a personal cruising experience—or explain the psychology behind this activity.

⊃ *Nice Surprise*

It's great when someone notices how *well* you're doing. When was the last time that happened to you? Recall such an occasion.

1.1 It was Friday night.
1.2 Tony was feeling good.

2.1 He had worked hard.
2.2 He had gotten a raise.
2.3 The raise was unexpected.

3.1 His boss had praised his efforts.
3.2 His boss was a hardworking woman.

4.1   Then she had handed him a paycheck.
4.2   The paycheck contained a bonus.
4.3   The bonus was small but worthwhile.

Then She handed in a PayCheck Which Contained
A Small but worthwhile Bonus.

5.1   He had said this to her.
5.2   "There must be some mistake."
5.3   She had just smiled.
5.4   She had assured him otherwise.

6.1   Tony liked the extra money.
6.2   The recognition pleased him even more.
6.3   The recognition acknowledged his efforts.

Tony liked the Extra Money, the Recognition
Pleased him ever More And acknowledged his Effort

7.1   Maybe his effort really mattered.
7.2   Maybe his attitude really mattered.
7.3   His job could be more than a meal ticket.

8.1   He had worked extra hard all week.
8.2   He hadn't thought anyone would notice.
8.3   Now he knew otherwise.

Writing Tip   Try combining cluster 5 with direct quotation and indirect quotation to see which approach you prefer.

Invitation   What lesson does this simple incident drive home? Develop your thoughts in a follow-up paragraph related to Tony or to yourself.

⊃ *Beauty Queen*

We often think "more is better." But maybe being *too* beautiful or *too* handsome poses a different set of problems.

1.1   Tonya was a woman.
1.2   She was stunningly beautiful.
1.3   She knew it.

2.1   Her face had classic proportions.
2.2   It had high cheekbones.
2.3   It had almond-shaped eyes.

3.1   Her jet-black hair glistened.
3.2   Her hair was long.
3.3   Her skin was clear.
3.4   Its clarity was flawless.

4.1   She moved through a crowd.
4.2   All heads turned.

5.1   She entered a noisy room.
5.2   People whispered in hushed tones.

6.1   Tonya resembled an Egyptian princess.
6.2   She had no close friends.
6.3   She had surprisingly few dates.

7.1   Everyone else was out having fun.
7.2   The Beauty Queen remained at home.
7.3   She considered her image in the mirror.

8.1   Perhaps other women envied her good looks.
8.2   Perhaps men feared her rejection.

Writing Tip   Try using *with* as a connector in cluster 2. Try adding an
-ly ending to *flawless* in cluster 3.

Invitation   Is there a two-sided problem here? Develop your own
thoughts on the problem of judging people by appearances.

⊃ *Parable 1*

You probably remember "The Tortoise and the Hare." Here's a similar sort
of tale with a different message.

1.1   A Fox saw a Crow.
1.2   The Crow was flying.
1.3   Crow had some cheese.
1.4   Her beak held the cheese.

2.1   Crow settled on a branch.
2.2   The branch was on a tree.

3.1   Fox wanted the cheese.
3.2   Fox approached the tree.
3.3   Fox spoke to Crow.
3.4   Fox called her Mistress Crow.

4.1 He complimented Crow.
4.2 She looked remarkably well.
4.3 Her feathers were glossy.
4.4 Her eyes were bright.

5.1 Fox then remarked on Crow's voice.
5.2 It was reported to have a sound.
5.3 The sound was sweet and melodious.

6.1 He asked Crow to sing one song.
6.2 He might call her Queen of the Birds.

7.1 Crow preened her black feathers.
7.2 Crow opened her mouth to caw.
7.3 Crow dropped the cheese.

8.1 Fox snapped up what he wanted.
8.2 That thing was the cheese.
8.3 Fox gave Crow some advice.
8.4 "Flatterers can't be trusted."

Writing Tip   Clusters 3, 7, and 8 provide contexts for you to use participles as openers (words like *wanting, preening,* and *snapping*). In what *other* ways can you combine these clusters?

Invitation   A parable is a brief tale that illustrates a lesson. Make up your own parable with whatever moral you want to teach.

ↄ *Parable 2*

Sometimes fables have more than one interpretation. Watch for different meanings as you combine sentences and think about Parable 2.

1.1   Sea gulls circle in the dawn.
1.2   The sea gulls are young.
1.3   The dawn is gray.
1.4   The dawn is drizzly.

2.1   The birds dip in the chill wind.
2.2   The birds soar in the chill wind.
2.3   Their wings are extended.
2.4   Then they swoop to earth together.

3.1   They are just in time for Flying School.
3.2   It tries to teach them about boats.
3.3   It tries to teach them about docks.
3.4   It tries to teach them about survival.

4.1   An old bird advises them.
4.2   "Stay close to shore!"
4.3   "Watch for human trash!"
4.4   "It drifts in with the waves!"

5.1   The gulls flap their wings.
5.2   The flapping is restless.
5.3   Their instructor reminds them.
5.4   They should forget their dreams.

6.1 The instructor adds this.
6.2 "Gulls must live in flocks!"
6.3 "Gulls must live close to the docks!"

7.1 "Gulls cannot fly high and free!"
7.2 "Flying would be above the sea."
7.3 "The sea is open and rolling."

8.1 The class follows the teacher.
8.2 The class searches for breakfast.
8.3 One bird lags behind.
8.4 One bird remembers a private dream.

Writing Tip As you combine, remember that quotation marks are placed outside of both commas and periods.

Invitation Explain the moral of the "Flying School" fable in a follow-up paragraph of interpretation. After making your own meaning, share with others and listen to their paragraphs.

➲ Picnic Lunch

Where do you go to get away from it all? Can you re-create the sensory details of this place so that your reader can know it?

1.1 The sun came off the water.
1.2 The sun glinted in the green eddies.
1.3 The sun glittered in the green eddies.

2.1 Around us were the sounds of insects.
2.2 Around us were the sounds of leaves.
2.3 The sounds were lazy.
2.4 The leaves were rustling.

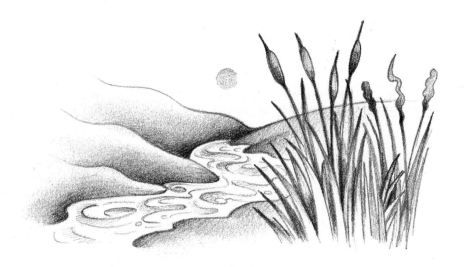

3.1 We skipped flat rocks.
3.2 The rocks bruised the water with splashes.
3.3 The splashes were white.

4.1 Then we edged along the river bank.
4.2 The bank was rocky.
4.3 The bank was thick with weeds.
4.4 The weeds were low-growing.

5.1 We ducked under willow branches.
5.2 The branches were overhanging.
5.3 We could smell the pines above.
5.4 We could smell juniper above.

6.1 Twigs crunched underfoot.
6.2 Pinecones crunched underfoot.
6.3 Birds cruised low across the river.

7.1 We savored the afternoon's warmth.
7.2 We savored the afternoon's quiet.
7.3 We hiked to an open grassy ridge.
7.4 It was where we could have lunch.

8.1 City noise was far away.
8.2 Diesel stench was far away.
8.3 A memory of final exams was far away.
8.4 This was at least for now.

Writing Tip   Note that you will need a plural verb as you combine cluster 8.

Invitation   Describe a favorite place that you like to visit, either alone or with someone else.

⊃ *Disney Pilgrims*

Religious people have made pilgrimages for centuries. Is it possible that our culture has produced a new kind of pilgrim?

1.1 Religious people make pilgrimages.
1.2 The pilgrimages are to confirm their faith.
1.3 The pilgrimages are to redeem themselves.

2.1 Jews visit the Wailing Wall, in Jerusalem.
2.2 Muslims journey to the holy city of Mecca.
2.3 Catholics try to get to Lourdes, in France.
2.4 Devout Mormons head for Salt Lake City.

3.1 A similar pilgrimage is to Disneyland.
3.2 A similar pilgrimage is to Disney World.
3.3 Millions of Americans undertake it each year.

4.1 These destinations serve as national shrines.
4.2 The shrines are for a secular religion.
4.3 The religion is known as "entertainment."

5.1 Pilgrims make offerings at the gate.
5.2 Pilgrims enter a city within a city.
5.3 It is called the "Magic Kingdom."
5.4 The "Magic Kingdom" is self-contained.

6.1 Cartoons come to life in this world.
6.2 One can actually see Mickey Mouse.
6.3 One can see other Disney creations.
6.4 One wanders among different "lands."

7.1 Pilgrims leave worldly cares behind.
7.2 They transcend the constraints of time.
7.3 They visit Tomorrowland.
7.4 They visit Main Street, U.S.A.

8.1 They finally leave the shrine.
8.2 They usually take home souvenirs.
8.3 The souvenirs serve as sacred relics.
8.4 The relics remind them of the pilgrimage.

Writing Tip In cluster 2, consider using semicolons (;) between each of the four clauses; use *and* before the last clause.

Invitation Does entertainment really serve a religious purpose in our society? Look for other examples, and write them up.

⊃ First Love

We all remember our first love—and our first kiss. Can you recall the situation as if it were yesterday? And was it?

1.1 Kevin felt tense.
1.2 Kevin felt unsure of himself.
1.3 Kevin edged closer to his date.
1.4 He sneaked a sideways look.

2.1 The movie theater was dark.
2.2 Her profile was still visible.
2.3 Her profile was backlighted.

3.1 He stared at her mouth.
3.2 Her mouth was full and inviting.
3.3 He swallowed his hesitation.
3.4 His hesitation was fearful.

4.1 Music began to swell.
4.2 The music was melodramatic.
4.3 The movie's intrigue heightened.

5.1 Kevin could hear his own breathing.
5.2 His breathing was labored.
5.3 Kevin told himself this.
5.4 "It's now or never."

6.1   There was a pause between them.
6.2   The pause was long.
6.3   The pause was breathless.
6.4   Nothing happened.

7.1   And then she tilted her head slightly.
7.2   The tilt was in his direction.
7.3   She lifted her chin.
7.4   She leaned back against his arm.
7.5   Her eyes were half-closed.

8.1   Kevin leaned forward.
8.2   Kevin helped himself to her popcorn.
8.3   Her popcorn was nearly all gone.

Writing Tip   Try using a *with* connector in sentence 7.5 after you delete the verb *were*.

Invitation   Take it from here with follow-up descriptive writing. Or, if you prefer, write about your own first kiss.

⊃ Hispanic Movement

The Hispanic Movement has helped shape the direction of American culture today. What is this movement? How does it work?

1.1   The Hispanic Movement results from efforts.
1.2   Mexican-Americans make the efforts.
1.3   The efforts are to assert identity.
1.4   The identity is cultural and political.

2.1   Hispanics now demand a voice in institutions.
2.2   The Hispanics are politically active.
2.3   The institutions affect their lives.

3.1 Hispanics seek to preserve their heritage.
3.2 Their heritage is a mix of Spanish traditions.
3.3 Their heritage is a mix of Indian traditions.
3.4 The mix is colorful.

4.1 Hispanics want to promote self-awareness.
4.2 They want to promote cooperation.
4.3 The cooperation is in their communities.
4.4 They want to promote ethnic pride.

5.1 One approach to such goals is Hispanic Studies.
5.2 These provide a context for studying history.
5.3 These provide a context for studying literature.
5.4 These provide a context for studying culture.

6.1 A second approach is Hispanic newspapers.
6.2 A second approach is Hispanic magazines.
6.3 These stimulate literary expression.
6.4 These provide a forum for an exchange of views.

7.1 A third approach is political action committees.
7.2 These express Hispanic concerns in elections.
7.3 These work in support of particular candidates.
7.4 These work in support of specific legislation.

8.1 Such efforts enable Hispanics to articulate aims.
8.2 Their aims are social.
8.3 Their aims are political.
8.4 Their aims are economic.
8.5 Such efforts enable Hispanics to achieve them.

Writing Tip Try parallelism in clusters 2, 3, and 4 and then in 5, 6, and 7. See "Parallelism in Sentences" in *Appendix B*, pages 221–224.

Invitation Describe a specific example of how the Hispanic Movement has affected your community or region for the better.

ↄ *Roadside Attraction*

Advertisers try to capture our attention. But what if their shock techniques pose safety hazards or assault the visual environment?

1.1 Billboards are a new kind of advertising medium.
1.2 The billboards are inflatable.
1.3 The advertising is along roadsides.

2.1 These signs capture one's attention.
2.2 The signs are three-dimensional.
2.3 The capture is dramatic.

3.1 For example, imagine a killer whale.
3.2 The whale is lifelike.
3.3 It appears to leap from a billboard.

4.1 Such a sight is not soon forgotten.
4.2 Its advertiser is not soon forgotten.
4.3 Its advertiser is Marineland.

5.1 Cars are also subjects for such displays.
5.2 Trucks are also subjects for such displays.
5.3 Boats are also subjects for such displays.

6.1 Models of this kind are made from fabric.
6.2 The fabric is woven nylon.
6.3 The fabric has been dipped in vinyl.
6.4 The vinyl is melted.

7.1 This fabric is virtually vandalproof.
7.2 It is extremely tough.
7.3 It has survived bullets.
7.4 It has survived arrows.

8.1 Small holes are no problem.
8.2 A fan keeps the billboard inflated.
8.3 The fan runs continuously.

Writing Tip   For subject-verb agreement in cluster 4, change *is* to *are*.
Try a *which* connector for cluster 7.

Invitation   Are inflatable billboards here to stay? How would
you argue for (or against) them in your community?

⊃ *Sassy Sauce*

Thanks to Mexican-American cuisine, many Americans now reach for salsa, the sauce that wakes up your mouth. How about you?

1.1 It's time to enjoy good food.
1.2 We Americans gather around.
1.3 We spread on the salsa.

2.1 We fold it into omelettes.
2.2 We put it on sandwiches for lunch.
2.3 We scoop it up with corn chips after work.

3.1 Mexican-American food has become popular.
3.2 Its popularity is throughout the United States.
3.3 Salsa has become the condiment of choice.
3.4 It now surpasses ketchup in total sales.

4.1 Pueblo Indians first created such sauces.
4.2 The Pueblo Indians live in the desert southwest.
4.3 The sauces combined chilies and tomatoes.

5.1 But news of good food travels fast.
5.2 Native Americans eventually shared their secrets.
5.3 The secrets were culinary.

6.1 Today's salsa usually sticks to the basics.
6.2 It may also include chopped onions and garlic.
6.3 It may also include green peppers and jalapeños.
6.4 It may perhaps even include cilantro.

7.1 Salsa is like its Hispanic and Indian heritage.
7.2 Salsa blends many ingredients into a flavor.
7.3 The flavor is memorable and distinctive.

8.1 Salsa is like Mexican-American culture today.
8.2 Salsa's flavor is difficult to resist.
8.3 Salsa's spiciness is difficult to resist.
8.4 Salsa's versatility is difficult to resist.

Writing Tip   Try beginning clusters 7 and 8 with the word *like*. Be sure to change *is* to *are* as you combine cluster 8 sentences.

Invitation   Develop a follow-up paragraph linked to the assertions in clusters 7 and 8 about Mexican-American culture.

⊃ *House Special*

"As American as apple pie" was the slogan of yesteryear. So what is today's standard? Burgers and fries, perhaps?

1.1   Slabs of meat hit the hot griddle.
1.2   The meat is grayish-pink.
1.3   The griddle is black.

2.1   Blood pops.
2.2   Blood sputters.
2.3   The patties sizzle in a puddle.
2.4   The puddle is greasy.

3.1   Rows of buns are slathered with mayonnaise.
3.2   The rows are orderly.
3.3   The mayonnaise is rich.
3.4   This is in preparation for burgers.
3.5   The burgers shrink steadily.

4.1   Fries are dumped into a basket.
4.2   The fries are frozen.
4.3   The basket is wire.
4.4   Fries are lowered into oil.
4.5   The lowering is slow.

5.1   Their bath foams.
5.2   Their bath crackles.
5.3   Their bath is 400 degrees.

6.1 The fries release clouds of steam.
6.2 The fries are thinly sliced.
6.3 The clouds are thick.
6.4 The steam is swirling.

7.1 The patties are eased into place.
7.2 The patties are grainy.
7.3 The patties are machine-stamped.
7.4 The sandwich is quickly wrapped.
7.5 The sandwich is ready for sale.

8.1 The nearby potatoes come out crisp.
8.2 The nearby potatoes come out golden.
8.3 They are dripping with oil.
8.4 The oil is hydrogenated.

Writing Tip Notice how adjectives can precede and follow nouns throughout this exercise. Experiment with adjective positioning.

Invitation Introduce your personal views, positive or negative, on the "House Special" diet. Or describe a favorite food as vividly as you can.

⊃ Breakfast Routine

For some people, breakfast means coffee and a cigarette. What do you think about such a life-style choice? Is it your cup of tea?

1.1 A young woman sits alone.
1.2 She sips from her coffee cup.
1.3 It is chipped along the rim.

2.1 The coffee's taste is acidic.
2.2 It is faintly soapy.

2.3   There is a brown film.
2.4   It is inside the cup.

3.1   She takes care not to spill the coffee.
3.2   It is rumored to eat holes in clothing.

4.1   This is done without thinking.
4.2   She finds a cigarette.
4.3   She scrapes a match into action.

5.1   It sputters into yellowish flame.
5.2   The sputtering is uneasy.
5.3   The flame wavers.
5.4   The flame licks its way up the matchstick.

6.1   Its death comes from cigarette smoke.
6.2   Its death is sudden.
6.3   The smoke is exhaled.

7.1 A wisp threads upward.
7.2 The wisp is curling.
7.3 It becomes part of the shadows.

8.1 The woman inhales deeply.
8.2 The woman tastes the coffee.
8.3 The woman considers today's problems.
8.4 The woman considers tomorrow's promises.

Writing Tip Try connectors like *because* and *which* in cluster 3. Try a connector like *that* in cluster 5.

Invitation Develop a follow-up paragraph that comments on this breakfast ritual by offering your personal views.

⊃ *No Sweat*

Like other Americans, you possess eight miles of sweat glands and will probably contribute to a $2 billion industry this year.

1.1 Human skin is a complex organ.
1.2 It is sometimes called the third kidney.
1.3 It helps us remove wastes through sweating.

2.1 Perspiration flushes away urea.
2.2 It flushes away lactic acid.
2.3 It flushes away toxic metals.
2.4 The metals include lead.
2.5 The metals include mercury.

3.1 This is contrary to popular belief.
3.2 Most sweat is actually odorless.
3.3 Humans cannot "sweat like a pig."

4.1 Any odor is created by bacteria.
4.2 Odor is associated with perspiration.
4.3 The bacteria are on the skin's surface.
4.4 Pigs do not have bodily sweat glands.

5.1 Pigs are like cats and dogs.
5.2 Pigs have sweat glands only on lips.
5.3 Pigs have sweat glands only on foot pads.
5.4 Pigs roll in the mud to keep cool.

6.1 We humans have over two million sweat glands.
6.2 These enable us to control body temperature.
6.3 We use the same cooling process as horses.
6.4 The process is perspiration.

7.1 Europeans once used scented handkerchiefs.
7.2 This was to deal with unwanted body odors.
7.3 Today's consumers turn to deodorants.
7.4 Today's consumers turn to antiperspirants.

8.1 Antiperspirants do present health risks.
8.2 They contain aluminum salts.
8.3 The aluminum salts close up sweat ducts.
8.4 Studies suggest a link with Alzheimer's disease.

Writing Tip For sentence variety, try opening clusters 3 and 5 with *contrary* and *like*, respectively. Try a colon in cluster 6.

Invitation Since researchers have found a trend toward higher risk of Alzheimer's disease with increased use of antiperspirants, should warning labels be required? Why or why not?

⊃ *Name Game*

How important is a name to a person's identity? Do you agree with Shakespeare that a rose is still a rose by any other name?

1.1   Bill Clinton was elected U.S. President.
1.2   Most Americans welcomed Hillary Clinton.
1.3   A majority did not welcome her preferred name.
1.4   The name is Hillary Rodham Clinton.

2.1   Debate on women's surnames goes back to 1855.
2.2   Lucy Stone was a passionate voice.
2.3   The voice opposed slavery.
2.4   The voice spoke out for women's rights.

3.1   Stone organized a first national convention.
3.2   The convention was on women's rights.
3.3   She also published *Woman's Journal.*
3.4   It was an influential periodical of the day.

4.1   She rejected marriage offers for years.
4.2   She eventually agreed to marry Henry Blackwell.
4.3   Blackwell shared her belief in equal rights.

5.1 Stone and Blackwell were married in 1855.
5.2 They formally protested the marriage laws.
5.3 The laws gave power and property to men.
5.4 They argued for marriage as a partnership.
5.5 The partnership was permanent and legal.

6.1 Their protest created a storm of controversy.
6.2 Many people were angered by Stone's decision.
6.3 The decision was to keep her own name.
6.4 It symbolized her individuality.

7.1 Stone won the right to the name of Stone.
7.2 She was later refused the right to vote.
7.3 The local registrar refused to recognize it.

8.1 Hillary Clinton's experience suggests this.
8.2 Attitudes toward women's roles die hard.
8.3 Attitudes toward women's surnames die hard.
8.4 The attitudes are traditional.

Writing Tip   In cluster 7, consider using short clauses for emphasis. In cluster 8, use *that* as a connector for combining.

Invitation   Use "Name Game" as a springboard for expressing your own views about women's surnames following marriage vows.

⊃ *Bait and Switch*

The weather is great, and you're in the mood to kick some tires on car lots. Who knows? Maybe you'll discover a great deal.

1.1 Many car dealers use a sales strategy.
1.2 The sales strategy is cunning.
1.3 The strategy is called "bait and switch."

2.1   The typical "bait" is a newspaper ad.
2.2   The consumer notices with surprise.
2.3   "This is too good to be true!"

3.1   The consumer may not notice something.
3.2   The car is always "subject to prior sale."
3.3   It often excludes important accessories.

4.1   The "switch" begins at the car lot.
4.2   The consumer inquires about the vehicle.
4.3   The consumer is eager to buy.
4.4   The vehicle was advertised.

5.1   The car's location is often a mystery.
5.2   The car's availability is often a mystery.
5.3   Sales reps usually have "similar cars."
5.4   The reps are happy to show these.
5.5   The reps are happy to talk about these.

6.1   An associate may "search" for the car.
6.2   The car is in question.
6.3   The sales rep gets acquainted.
6.4   The sales rep makes small talk.

7.1   The rep engages the prospect in conversation.
7.2   This is to begin "the switch."
7.3   The conversation is about "car needs."
7.4   The conversation is about "desired features."

8.1   The rep is now armed with information.
8.2   The rep works for "the switch."
8.3   The rep invites consideration of another car.
8.4   This one is "also marked down for today only."

Writing Tip   Notice how quotation marks are used throughout this exercise to make the reader critically aware. Remember to place quotation marks *outside* commas and periods.

Invitation Recall a situation in which you negotiated, or tried to negotiate, with a seller on some important purchase. Set the scene clearly, and tell the story.

⊃ *Hurricane Behavior*

Hurricanes devastated Florida and the island of Kauai in 1992. How were these storms formed?

1.1 The tropics supply hot weather.
1.2 The tropics supply warm oceans.
1.3 The tropics supply a thunderstorm.
1.4 These are basic ingredients for a hurricane.

2.1 The hurricane begins as a thunderstorm.
2.2 The thunderstorm is harmless.
2.3 It forms off the coast of west Africa.

3.1 Easterly winds carry it over tropical waters.
3.2 The waters have been heated by the summer sun.
3.3 Rising heat begins to energize the storm.
3.4 Rising heat causes it to grow.

4.1 Lightning bolts flash.
4.2 Winds begin to circulate and howl.
4.3 The storm becomes more powerful.

5.1 Evaporating water causes heavier rains.
5.2 The rains release heat and energy.
5.3 This, in turn, creates a low-pressure center.
5.4 The center is called the hurricane's "eye."

6.1 The storm forms a circle of wind.
6.2 The circle is tightly knit.

6.3   The circle swirls counterclockwise.
6.4   The circle is like a spinning top.

7.1   The sea rises under the hurricane's eye.
7.2   The eye is low-pressure.
7.3   This creates a "storm surge."
7.4   The "storm surge" is highly destructive.

8.1   The hurricane moves ashore.
8.2   It pushes a wall of water.
8.3   The wall may reach twenty feet high.
8.4   This is not counting the waves on top.

Writing Tip   Try a dash for emphasis when combining cluster 1 and cluster 8. Try a semicolon when combining cluster 5.

Invitation   Describe a physical process that you know something about—for example, programming a VCR. Imagine as your audience a person who does not know how to do this task.

➲ *Cramming for Exams*

Is it possible that American colleges and universities coddle students in basic ways? Combine and make up your own mind!

1.1   Americans often cram for quizzes.
1.2   Americans often cram for exams.
1.3   Students in Europe distribute their studying.
1.4   Distribution tends to integrate learning.

2.1   Patterns of assessment cause such differences.
2.2   The patterns are contrasting.
2.3   The differences are dramatic.
2.4   The differences are in student behavior.

3.1   American schools employ continuous assessment.
3.2   Continuous assessment assumes something.
3.3   Students do not enjoy studying.
3.4   Students must therefore be monitored.
3.5   The monitoring is on a regular basis.

4.1   Instructors set up a schedule of quizzes.
4.2   Instructors set up a schedule of exams.
4.3   Students organize their studying accordingly.
4.4   They often put off their reading.
4.5   They often cram at the last minute.

5.1   This pattern differs from the European model.
5.2   It may test students at year's end.
5.3   It may delay testing for two or more years.

6.1   European students understand something.
6.2   A process of cramming is useless.
6.3   They must organize their own time.
6.4   They must discipline themselves to study.

7.1   Students have one chance to pass an exam.
7.2   They take the exam seriously.
7.3   So much of their future rides on its results.

8.1   The American system rewards students for cramming.
8.2   The European model rewards genuine learning.

Writing Tip   Use a contrast connector (such as *but, however, whereas, although,* or *while*) in clusters 1 and 8. Notice that this paragraph is built on the principle of contrast.

Invitation   (1) Develop a paragraph contrasting your study habits in high school and college, or (2) explain why American colleges should (or should not) adopt the European model.

⊃ A Man with Heart

Medicine involves human stories, often in life-and-death situations. Consider, for example, the first heart surgery.

1.1   Dr. Dan Williams was put to the test in 1893.
1.2   This was ten years after getting his medical degree.
1.3   This was two years after founding Provident Hospital.
1.4   Provident was the nation's first interracial facility.

2.1   A young black man had been stabbed in a bar fight.
2.2   Williams was called upon to examine the chest wound.
2.3   Williams was then Provident's chief surgeon.

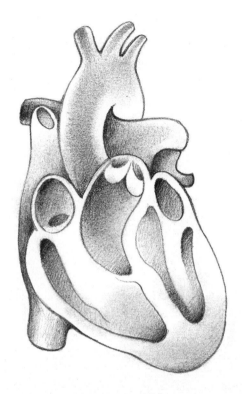

3.1 The man became pale.
3.2 The man developed a sharp cough.
3.3 Williams suspected internal bleeding.
3.4 The bleeding could be from a heart wound.

4.1 Cold packs was the usual treatment in such cases.
4.2 A painkiller was the usual treatment in such cases.
4.3 Rest was the usual treatment in such cases.
4.4 The patient almost always died.

5.1 Williams hoped to save the man's life.
5.2 Williams made his incision into the man's chest.
5.3 He discovered a bleeding blood vessel.
5.4 He promptly tied this off to stop its bleeding.

6.1 Even more serious was the tear in the pericardium.
6.2 The pericardium is the sac surrounding the heart.
6.3 The pericardium fluttered at 130 times per minute.

7.1 Williams cleaned the wound with a saline solution.
7.2 Williams sewed the edges together as best he could.
7.3 Williams then closed the outer incision.

8.1 The black man survived his historic operation.
8.2 The operation was the first heart surgery ever.
8.3 Dan Williams later found himself a very famous man.
8.4 Dan Williams was the black surgeon with heart.

Writing Tip Change *was* to *were* as you combine cluster 4. For sentence variety, try opening cluster 5 with *hoping.* Try dashes for emphasis in cluster 8.

Invitation The founding of the interracial hospital by Williams led to the creation of 40 similar facilities in 20 states. If Williams did this *then,* what seems important for you to do *now?*

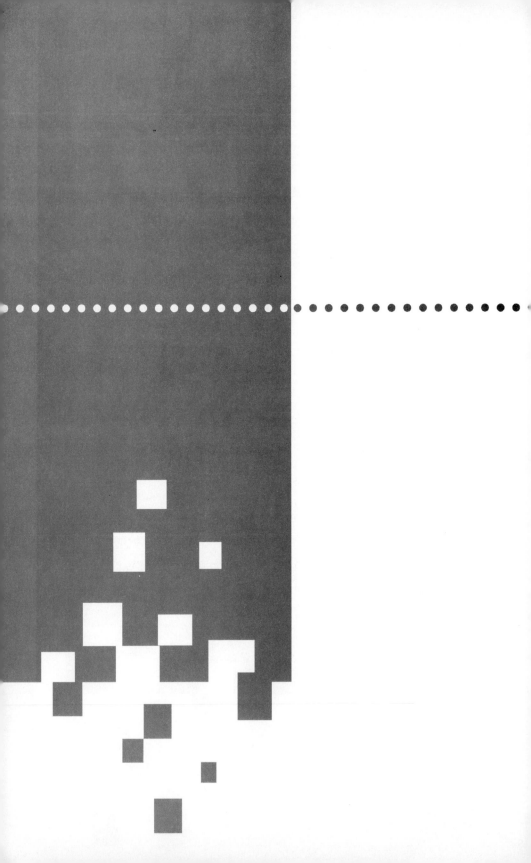

Intermediate Combining

Have you ever watched someone learning how to drive—or been through that process yourself? Can you recall your frustration with the strange commands and graphics of a new computer? Or the difficulty of learning to speak a second language?

Each of these examples reminds us that new learning often takes tremendous energy. Such events stand out in our minds *because* we had such difficulty with them. And yet soon after we learn a complex set of habits, we become virtually unaware of separate actions—like starting the car, shifting, braking, signaling to change lanes, or parallel parking. What was once difficult is now easy. Somehow, we're on "automatic pilot."

This same transformation—from difficult to easy, from *conscious* attention to *automatic* behavior—also happens when people extend their writing skills. Understanding how you learn writing will help you to be both patient and efficient as you practice sentence combining, respond to writing invitations, and work with others in writing groups.

TRAINING YOUR AUTOMATIC PILOT

Strange as it may seem, everyone has many automatic pilots, each trained to take over when its task comes up. In addition, everyone has pilots-in-training. For example, your pilot for using a knife and fork may be highly skilled, while the one for using chopsticks may be a bit uncertain, needing more experience with Asian foods. Of course, the *reverse* may also be true.

Similarly, you may have a well-trained pilot for driving the baseline and shooting jump shots but a lousy one for returning a tennis ball. The problem is not that your tennis pilot is asleep or on vacation; rather, this pilot simply needs more practice. Thousands of dribbles and baseline jumpers have put your basketball pilot on "automatic" when you hit the court.

Another well-trained pilot—regardless of your eating utensils or your basketball prowess—is the one that governs talk in your native language. Think about the countless utterances you must have heard from parents, siblings, friends, and the TV set when you were an infant and a small child. You were awash in language.

It's amazing but true: your language pilot was a phenomenally quick learner. At six months, you automatically made the sounds of your native language, not some other tongue. At nine months to a year, you used single words and pointed to engage others in conversations. At 18 months, you were making sentences. At 24 months, you combined ideas mentally and expressed them. And by age five or so, you had mastered all the basic sentence patterns and simple ways of combining. That self-programming of your brain computer has not been matched by today's supercomputers!

Was all of this easy? No. Adults would walk by your crib and hear you babbling to yourself—gooing and cooing at first, then saying words or phrases or rhymes. You were doing homework *all* the time, even when someone laid you down for nap. It was this virtually nonstop practice that trained your language pilot so quickly and thoroughly.

As a consequence, you don't have to think about *how* to talk in your native tongue. You simply do it. What you *think* about, probably, is content—making your meanings come across. Almost instantly, your language pilot takes over, expressing your ideas in the unique sounds, rhythms, and patterns you have mastered.

A PILOT FOR WRITING

You can see from the points above why an automatic pilot is so important: *it frees your mind to do other things.* Just as a pilot for talking allows you to focus on your message, so a pilot for writing frees you to think about *content* (what you're writing about), *organization* (how your message is structured), and *audience* (what they already know and need to know).

But as we noted earlier, training a pilot to go on automatic isn't always easy. It not only takes time and patience but also requires *attention* and *practice*. With sentence combining, daily practice leads to the quickest results in your own writing.

What sort of attention is important? As you combine ideas, begin to notice *sentence openers.* Do you always open sentences in the same way—or do you vary them occasionally? Also, be alert to your routines for *adding modifiers* and *using connectors.* How does your usual approach compare with those of other students? Finally, begin to use *terms and concepts* from Appendix A and Appendix B as you look at your own writing and the efforts of your workshop partners. Are you fully aware of your options?

A second kind of attention comes from your reading. Do you ever reread especially interesting sentences or copy them into your SC notebook (or portfolio)? What matters is that the content (or form) of certain sentences excites you. Perhaps a sentence eloquently voices the need for prenatal health care or expresses ethnic pride. Whatever the topic, self-selected sentences like these help your writing pilot train itself in sentence construction. Such copied-down patterns, soon internalized, will emerge automatically as you write more and more.

A basic aim of combining and copying sentences is to help you acquire an automatic pilot for sentence construction. When you make written sentences automatically, you free up energy and cognitive space for planning, among other things. As a result, writing becomes easier as well as more fun.

Think back to our driving analogy, and relate it to writing. When driving becomes automatic, you can concentrate on strategies (like mentally planning your route for several errands) rather than details (like shifting gears). Equally important, your automatic pilot frees you to enjoy the pleasure of trees coming into bloom or the sounds of a favorite FM station.

The same thing is true with writing. Increased ease with sentences frees you to think strategically about your writing. For one thing, you can create a mental map to explore a topic. For another, you can organize the beginning, middle, and end of your trip. And finally, an automatic pilot helps you get back on the main road after you've encountered unexpected detours.

⊃ *Vietnam Veterans Memorial*

Dedicated in 1982, the Vietnam Veterans Memorial is the most visited site in Washington, D.C. What is the attraction?

1.1 The Memorial lies in Constitution Gardens.
1.2 The Memorial is a wide V-shaped wall.

2.1 The wall is made of black granite.
2.2 The wall seems to rise from the earth.
2.3 The wall seems to recede into it.

3.1 Entering the Memorial is a moving experience.
3.2 The wall is inscribed with over 58,000 names.
3.3 Each refers to an American man or woman.
3.4 The man or woman was lost in Vietnam.

4.1 One sees line after line of American names.
4.2 These stretch for 250 feet in two directions.
4.3 The enormity of the nation's loss becomes clear.

5.1 The average age was nineteen.
5.2 The age was for soldiers killed in Vietnam.

5.3 Marines suffered a casualty rate of 24 percent.
5.4 This was for soldiers killed or wounded.

6.1 The wall is a place of quiet commemoration.
6.2 People come to acknowledge sacrifice here.
6.3 People come to remember a young face here.
6.4 People come to express private grief here.

7.1 And it would not exist except for one man.
7.2 This was a Vietnam veteran named Jan Scruggs.
7.3 He saw half of his company killed or wounded.
7.4 He barely escaped with his life.

8.1 Scruggs wanted to remember his comrades.
8.2 He wanted the nation to honor their commitment.
8.3 The nation had been divided over the Vietnam War.
8.4 The division had been bitter.

9.1 In 1979 he became obsessed with the project.
9.2 He began work to establish a Memorial Fund.
9.3 He began work to secure congressional approval.
9.4 The approval was for the concept of a memorial.

10.1 President Carter signed a bill in July 1980.
10.2 The bill authorized the Memorial.
10.3 The bill provided a site for it.
10.4 Scruggs's campaign moved into high gear.
10.5 The campaign was to raise private funds.

Writing Tip Look for opportunities to use (but not overuse) connectors such as *who, which,* and *that* in this exercise.

Invitation Great controversy surrounded the use of polished black granite, which mirrors trees, sky, earth, and the people who visit the Memorial. Why was black probably a good choice?

⊃ *Gambling Fever*

Before 1989, just two states—Nevada and New Jersey—had casino gambling. Now 11 more states have some form of legalized gambling. Why?

1.1 State budgets are tight.
1.2 Taxpayers are in open revolt.
1.3 Legalized gambling generates huge profits.
1.4 Profits can support government services.

2.1 Gross revenues in 1991 exceeded $26 billion.
2.2 This compares with $5 billion from receipts.
2.3 The receipts are in the film industry.

3.1 Thirty-two states have lotteries.
3.2 The lotteries are operated by the government.
3.3 The lotteries siphon about $17 billion.
3.4 This is used to support various programs.
3.5 The programs often include education.

4.1 Over 50 Indian tribes also run casinos.
4.2 Over 50 Indian tribes also run bingo games.
4.3 These cannot be regulated by the states.
4.4 This is because of a Supreme Court ruling.

5.1 Gambling on reservations grossed $6 billion.
5.2 This amount was split with 17 states in 1991.
5.3 Some cities may now *give* land to Indian tribes.
5.4 This is in exchange for future gambling revenues.

6.1 Yet gambling raises serious moral questions.
6.2 Lawmakers rarely consider moral questions.
6.3 They face problems with government budgets.

7.1 Gambling exploits people from the inner cities.
7.2 The gambling is state-sponsored.
7.3 These people are vulnerable to messages.
7.4 The messages are slick and tantalizing.
7.5 The messages promise a better life.

8.1 Consider an example.
8.2 The example is an Illinois lottery billboard.
8.3 The billboard is in a Chicago ghetto.
8.4 "This Could Be Your Ticket Out."

9.1 Lottery sales soar in poor neighborhoods.
9.2 People are often hungry and desperate.
9.3 They are ill-equipped to understand the odds.
9.4 The odds underlie their participation.

10.1 Gambling may provide entertainment for many.
10.2 The entertainment is harmless.
10.3 It may also undermine our value system.
10.4 It promotes a dream of "something for nothing."
10.5 It promotes a dream of "wealth without work."

Writing Tip In cluster 5, consider a semicolon + *therefore* for sentence variety. Try the same pattern with *however* in cluster 10.

Invitation   Does legalized gambling represent government's cynical approach for taxing the poor? Or is it a good way to raise extra revenue? Take a stand, and express your viewpoint.

⊃ *Pumped Up*

You've seen muscle magazines on the newsstands—ones that reach a readership of 7 million Americans who want to be "pumped up."

1.1   No one wants to be a 97-pound weakling.
1.2   This is especially true for young American men.
1.3   They have seen Rambo and Terminator films.
1.4   These present "macho" images of strength.

2.1   Adolescents are inspired by images from TV.
2.2   Adolescents are inspired by muscle magazines.
2.3   Adolescents have created a bodybuilding subculture.
2.4   It often uses steroids to achieve results.

3.1   The black market for steroids is enormous.
3.2   It supplies 1 million users with drugs.
3.3   Half of this number are teenagers.
3.4   It grosses at least $400 million annually.

4.1   Steroids can stunt a person's growth.
4.2   Steroids may lead to liver problems.
4.3   Steroids may lead to kidney problems.
4.4   Most men start using "juice" before age 16.
4.5   Some start as early as age 10.

5.1   Overdoses of growth hormone can cause acromegaly.
5.2   Acromegaly is called "Frankenstein's Syndrome."
5.3   This condition distorts the face.

5.4 This condition distorts hands and feet.
5.5 This condition eventually leads to death.

6.1 Equally serious are psychological mood swings.
6.2 Cycles of steroid use create the mood swings.

7.1 Steroid users often experience depressions.
7.2 They are not using the drugs.
7.3 This pattern typically leads to increased use.

8.1 "Juicers" may have feelings of euphoria.
8.2 The euphoria is invincible.
8.3 Irritability often accompanies the "pump."
8.4 An urge to fight often accompanies the "pump."

9.1 Such aggression can lead to vandalism.
9.2 Such aggression can lead to assaults.
9.3 Such aggression can lead even to murder.
9.4 It is sometimes fueled by delusions.
9.5 It is sometimes fueled by paranoia.

10.1 Over 80 percent of teenagers believe something.
10.2 Steroids are completely harmless.
10.3 Half this number would continue their use.
10.4 This was even if they were convinced otherwise.

Writing Tip For sentence variety, try opening cluster 2 with *inspired* and cluster 8 with *while*. Also, be sure to check subject-verb agreement as you combine cluster 8.

Invitation No federal money has been spent studying the long-term health effects of steroids. How would you convince federal officials that the study of steroids should become a priority?

⊃ *Nuclear Waste*

The partial meltdown at Three Mile Island in 1979 and the disaster of Chernobyl in 1986 alerted U.S. citizens to the dangers of the nuclear age. Here's yet another threat.

1.1 Over 25 nations have nuclear power plants.
1.2 The nations include the United States.
1.3 The plants have produced tons of waste.
1.4 The waste is radioactive.

2.1 This waste poses a threat to civilization.
2.2 This waste poses a threat to the environment.
2.3 The threat is extraordinarily serious.
2.4 Its radiation is so lethal.
2.5 Its radiation is so long-lasting.

3.1 Nuclear waste eventually becomes harmless.
3.2 The process can take 10,000 years to achieve.

4.1 Radioactive wastes cannot be burned.
4.2 Radioactive wastes cannot be discarded.
4.3 Ways must be found to contain them.
4.4 The containment must be permanent.

5.1 Such wastes are now stored in facilities.
5.2 The facilities are temporary.
5.3 These include "ponds" at power plants.
5.4 These include underground steel tanks.
5.5 The tanks are on selected federal lands.

6.1 About 50,000 metric tons will accumulate.
6.2 The accumulation is high-level wastes.
6.3 The wastes will be mostly in solid form.
6.4 This will be in the United States alone.
6.5 This will be by the year 2000.

7.1 High-level waste generates great heat.
7.2 It emits deadly forms of radiation.
7.3 It must be handled by equipment, not humans.

8.1 Shielding can be provided by lead.
8.2 Shielding can be provided by concrete.
8.3 Shielding can be provided by steel.
8.4 Shielding can be provided by water.
8.5 The shielding is temporary.

9.1 Underground burial presents problems.
9.2 The problems are technical.
9.3 The rock must not melt from intense heat.
9.4 The rock surrounds the radioactive waste.
9.5 The waste generates intense heat.

10.1 Another hazard is groundwater.
10.2 Water might first leak into a burial site.
10.3 It might cause canisters to leak.
10.4 It might then carry radiation into aquifers.
10.5 The aquifers are underground.

Writing Tip   In clusters 2, 4, and 7, try using different cause-and-effect connectors—words and phrases such as *because, so, since, therefore, consequently,* and *as a result.*

Invitation   Some Third World countries in Latin America and Africa have agreed to store hazardous wastes because of their desperate poverty. Should our country export its wastes elsewhere?

⊃ *Magical Names*

Do you have a nickname or know someone who does? Where do you suppose the idea of nicknames came from?

1.1 We humans have spliced genes.
1.2 We humans have split the atom.
1.3 Names still exert magical power over us.

2.1 We feel uneasy with names like *cancer*.
2.2 We feel uneasy with names like *death*.
2.3 We therefore resort to euphemisms.
2.4 We therefore resort to substitutes.

3.1 We take offense at certain ethnic names.
3.2 We also take pride in other labels.
3.3 The labels change from time to time.

4.1 We invoke the names of supernatural beings.
4.2 The invocation depends on our religion.
4.3 The invocation is through prayers.
4.4 We utter oaths to damn our enemies.

5.1 Such modern examples recall an earlier time.
5.2 A name was a real part of one's identity then.
5.3 It was not just an identifying label.

6.1 A new son or daughter was born.
6.2 The child's name had to be kept secret.
6.3 A stranger might hear the name.
6.4 A stranger might use it to bewitch the child.

7.1 Nicknames grew from this widespread custom.
7.2 The custom was concealing one's true name.
7.3 The concealment was for reasons of security.

8.1 Our ancestors believed something.
8.2 Names invoked spirits.
8.3 The spirits were both good and bad.
8.4 Great care was exercised in name selection.

9.1 Christians often used the Bible as a guide.
9.2 Christians would open the book randomly.
9.3 Christians would glance down.
9.4 Christians would choose the first name.
9.5 The name was appropriate to the child's sex.

10.1 Superstitions about names persist today.
10.2 Parents often name children after leaders.
10.3 Parents often name children after entertainers.
10.4 Parents avoid the names of heinous criminals.

Writing Tip   Try a semicolon + *however* in cluster 1. Try a *because* connector as an opener for clusters 2 and 8.

Invitation   What do you know about the history of your name? Were you named after someone? Does your name carry certain family expectations? Why do you like (or dislike) your name?

⊃ *Man's World*

In the United States today, women assert influence in all professions—but such was not always the case. Read on.

1.1 Women were often second-class citizens.
1.2 This was during the nineteenth century.
1.3 Men controlled the positions of power.

2.1 Elizabeth Blackwell was a successful teacher.
2.2 She studied on her own to gain background.
2.3 The background would support her application.
2.4 Her application was to medical school.

3.1   Eleven schools rejected her application.
3.2   Geneva Medical College finally accepted her.
3.3   She graduated from there in 1849.
3.4   This was after much debate among the faculty.

4.1   The *Boston Medical Journal* made comments.
4.2   The comments were negative and critical.
4.3   The comments followed her graduation.
4.4   It said that she had overstepped her bounds.
4.5   These were set "by the order of nature."
4.6   These were set "by the common consent of the world."

5.1   She was rejected by all American hospitals.
5.2   Ms. Blackwell was forced to travel abroad.
5.3   The travel was to complete her medical work.

6.1   She returned to New York in 1851.
6.2   She had trouble finding office space.
6.3   No one would rent to a female physician.

7.1   Finally, she was forced to buy her own house.
7.2   She set up a small practice there.
7.3   The practice was successful.

8.1   By 1857 her practice had expanded.
8.2   It became the New York Infirmary for Women & Children.
8.3   It was the first hospital to be staffed by women.
8.4   It was one that offered medical internships.
8.5   The internships were for women students.

9.1   The struggle had been difficult.
9.2   Elizabeth Blackwell changed a man's world.
9.3   The change was for the better.

Writing Tip   For sentence variety, consider *rejected* as a sentence opener for cluster 5. Experiment with different *contrast* connectors for clusters 3 and 9.

Invitation Develop a profile of a woman who has made a breakthrough in law, education, the arts, broadcasting, sports, entertainment, or another profession.

⊃ *Ladies' Man*

Perhaps you've known a person like Alex, one who seems totally self-absorbed. Does Alex have a female counterpart?

1.1 Alex is a ladies' man.
1.2 He is smooth-talking.
1.3 He likes to wear aloha shirts.
1.4 The aloha shirts are open-collared.
1.5 He likes to wear thick gold chains.

2.1 He has a smile.
2.2 His smile is well practiced.
2.3 He has eyes.
2.4 His eyes are heavy-lidded.
2.5 His eyes are seductive.

3.1 His manner is suave.
3.2 His chatter is glib.
3.3 His grooming is impeccable.

4.1 He wears sexy jeans.
4.2 The jeans fit tightly.
4.3 He moves with grace.
4.4 His movement is suggestive.
4.5 His grace is undulating.

5.1 A mane of hair gives him a look.
5.2 The mane is thick.
5.3 The hair is black and shaggy.
5.4 The look is predatory.

6.1 He hangs out at the health club.
6.2 He swaggers among the weight machines.
6.3 He eyes himself in the mirrors.
6.4 The mirrors are full-length.
6.5 He flirts with ladies in the aerobics class.

7.1 Alex may have problems.
7.2 The problems are psychological.
7.3 Timidity is not among them.
7.4 Introversion is not among them.

8.1 At noon he heads for work.
8.2 This is after sculpting his hair.
8.3 Sculpting is with a blow dryer.
8.4 His work is at a car dealership.
8.5 He trolls for unwary customers.

Writing Tip   Make sure to check verb tense (changing *is* to *are*) as you combine sentences 7.3 and 7.4.

Invitation   Create another character sketch, with details like those in "Ladies' Man." Consider linking that sketch to this one.

⊃ *Championship Play-off*

The final moments of a championship game can provide a dramatic backdrop for narration. Watch how the action unfolds here.

1.1 Angie took a deep breath.
1.2 She approached the foul line.
1.3 Her teammates were gathered there.
1.4 They were urging her to relax.

2.1 She bounced the ball twice.
2.2 She fingered the seams.

2.3 She tried to concentrate on the basket.

2.4 She tried to ignore the deficit.

2.5 The deficit was two points.

2.6 There was only a minute to play.

3.1 Then she went into a slight crouch.

3.2 She drew the ball inward and up.

3.3 She lofted it toward the glass.

4.1 It struck the front rim.

4.2 It bounced high.

4.3 The players went up for the rebound.

4.4 The players were a tangle of arms.

4.5 The players were a tangle of elbows.

5.1 Marie came down with it.

5.2 She wheeled toward the outside.

5.3 She flicked it back to Angie.

5.4 Angie had dropped into the key.

6.1 The crowd was on its feet.

6.2 It screamed, "Shoot! Shoot!"

7.1 Angie drove past a defender.
7.2 Her body angled toward the baseline.
7.3 She shoveled a pass to Marie.
7.4 Marie had moved into the clear.

8.1 Marie faked upward.
8.2 This forced her opponent to jump.
8.3 Marie flicked the ball above fingertips.
8.4 The fingertips were outstretched.
8.5 The fingertips were desperate.

9.1 Its spin rippled the net.
9.2 Its spin was high and soft.
9.3 Its spin tied the score at 78.

10.1 The crowd became one giant voice.
10.2 It was an expanding balloon of sound.

Writing Tip   Clusters 4 and 10 provide opportunities for you to make appositives after the words *players* and *voice*.

Invitation   Continue the narrative action of the championship play-off, describing what happens in the next 42 seconds.

⊃ *Ancient Struggle*

Both humans and animals hunt to stay alive. What is your stand on hunting or fishing for sport—that is, for entertainment?

1.1 The fisherman waded out into the stream.
1.2 The stream was cold and fast-flowing.
1.3 The fisherman picked his way over rocks.
1.4 The rocks were slippery.

2.1 He used his fly rod as a wand.
2.2 He made great singing loops with his line.
2.3 He aimed for a deep hole downstream.

3.1 The current took his fly.
3.2 It disappeared in the river's shadows.
3.3 Its disappearance was sudden.
3.4 The shadows were green.

4.1 A trout came out of the water.
4.2 It was fighting to shake the hook.
4.3 The hook had been concealed in its supper.
4.4 It then headed for safety downstream.
4.5 It was making a run for it.

5.1 The fisherman worked it closer.
5.2 The fish surfaced again in the sunlight.
5.3 It thrashed its tail across the water.
5.4 It danced its tail across the water.

6.1 It headed off a third time.
6.2 It was still full of fight.
6.3 The fisherman bent down with his net.

7.1 It had been a fierce struggle.
7.2 It had been a noble struggle.
7.3 The fisherman knew his craft.
7.4 The fishman knew his equipment.

8.1 He reached down with care.
8.2 He released the barbless hook.
8.3 He admired the trout's wildness.
8.4 His wildness was sleek and silvery.
8.5 He released it back into the stream.

Writing Tip Try using *participial phrases*—with verb forms that end in *-ing*—to show the interplay of fisherman and fish.

Invitation Use "Ancient Struggle" as an opener to introduce your views on hunting and fishing as recreational activities.

⊃ *Air Pollution*

Air quality is a major problem in many cities. What specific ideas do you have to reduce the pollution of our air?

1.1   Air quality has reached a point of crisis.
1.2   This is in many American cities.
1.3   It now affects human health.
1.4   The effects are adverse.

2.1   Specialists predict something.
2.2   The specialists study the atmosphere.
2.3   The specialists study the environment.
2.4   Inaction will result in disaster.

3.1   Many will die because of "inversions."
3.2   The inversions trap carbon monoxide.
3.3   The inversions trap filthy air.
3.4   The trap is near the ground.

4.1 Legislators must pass laws.
4.2 The laws carry penalties for polluters.
4.3 The penalties are stiff.

5.1 Industries must comply with measures.
5.2 The measures are preventive.
5.3 Industries must decrease their discharge.
5.4 The discharge is atmospheric emissions.

6.1 Auto manufacturers must step up research.
6.2 The research is on engines.
6.3 The engines are clean-burning.
6.4 The engines are fuel-efficient.
6.5 The research is on pollution control.

7.1 Education efforts must be undertaken.
7.2 This is to promote conservation among citizens.
7.3 The citizens waste electric power.
7.4 The citizens burn trash illegally.
7.5 The citizens ignore public transportation.
7.6 The citizens buy oversized automobiles.

8.1 Such an approach must begin now.
8.2 The approach is coordinated.
8.3 The approach depends on public awareness.
8.4 Tomorrow is too late.

Writing Tip   In cluster 2, use *that* as a connector. In cluster 7, check punctuation for items in a series.

Invitation   Should gas be rationed? Should cities be closed to private cars? Should people who use public transportation get tax breaks? Should we build bicycle paths? Write up your idea.

⊃ *Summer Rain*

The afternoon is hot and sticky, a little like a steam bath. Maybe we need a summer rain to wash the air and refresh the spirit.

1.1 A wind begins building in the west.
1.2 The wind is warm and gusty.
1.3 The trees respond like dancers.
1.4 They bend and sway across the sky.

2.1 Above the mountains are clouds.
2.2 The clouds are fat and grayish.

2.3 The clouds scud across the horizon. *and*
2.4 They rub their underbellies on the peaks.

3.1 The sky darkens to a soft purple.
3.2 The ~~purple~~ is the color of plums.
3.3 The ~~plums are~~ now ripening in the trees.

4.1 A sudden hush gentles the wind. *and*
4.2 The trees suddenly go still.
4.3 Their branches are outstretched.
4.4 Their branches are awaiting the next act.

5.1 The sky now looks more ominous. *and*
5.2 The ~~sky now looks~~ more threatening. *like*
5.3 ~~It looks~~ like a bruise.
5.4 ~~The bruise is~~ large and painful.

6.1 A child looks up from her sidewalk play. *and*
6.2 She stares at trees. *that*
6.3 The trees no longer whisper. *nor*
6.4 The trees no longer dance.

7.1 And then she feels the first raindrops.
7.2 They are light and wet on her arm.
7.3 They are like unsure teardrops.

8.1 She lifts her small face.
8.2 She closes her eyes. *and*
8.3 She hears the rain come like a wave.

Writing Tip In cluster 3, try making an appositive—a renaming phrase like this.

Invitation Describe how the rain looks—hitting the sidewalk, dry soil, mud puddles—as well as how it sounds and smells.

⊃ *Japanese Business*

Although Japan lost World War II, it ranks as a leading economic power today. How did Japanese business achieve such success?

1.1 Japanese society encourages trust.
1.2 It also encourages cooperation.
1.3 This allows enterprises to flourish.
1.4 The enterprises are large corporations.

2.1 Japanese companies emphasize planning.
2.2 The planning is long-range.
2.3 Japanese companies emphasize consensus.
2.4 The consensus is in decision making.

3.1 Such companies are based on loyalties.
3.2 The loyalties are strong.
3.3 The loyalties are mutual.
3.4 Loyalties are between workers and employers.

4.1 Workers share in company profits.
4.2 They receive biannual bonuses.
4.3 This is when times are good.

5.1 They receive pay cuts.
5.2 They still keep their jobs.
5.3 This is when times are bad.

6.1 Promotions come slowly in Japanese firms.
6.2 Executives make commitments.
6.3 The commitments are for a lifetime.
6.4 Executives do not switch companies.

7.1 Specialization is a foreign concept.
7.2 Company leaders move among departments.
7.3 This is to understand the operations of the company.
7.4 Their understanding is complete.

8.1 Cooperation characterizes Japanese business.
8.2 Sacrifice characterizes Japanese business.
8.3 Teamwork characterizes Japanese business.
8.4 Japan has enjoyed dynamic growth since 1950.

Writing Tip Try connectors such as *because, so, therefore,* and *consequently* in clusters 6, 7, and 8. See "Parallelism in Sentences" in Appendix B, pages 221–224.

Invitation What change, if any, should occur in American business practice? Link your writing to the "Japanese Business" paragraph.

⊃ *Final Exam*

Has an instructor ever thrown you a curve in a final exam? Did you panic? Recall an occasion when the exam really surprised you.

1.1 Kathy slouched at her desk.
1.2 She chewed a fingernail nervously.
1.3 She stared at the final exam.
1.4 The exam was for her sociology course.

2.1 She could picture the first day of the course.
2.2 The instructor had introduced herself.
2.3 The instructor had explained the syllabus.
2.4 The syllabus called for independent thinking.
2.5 The syllabus called for creative thinking.

3.1 Kathy had read such statements before.
3.2 The statements were high-minded.
3.3 She knew from experience what really counted.
3.4 What counted were correct margins on papers.
3.5 What counted were noncontroversial opinions.
3.6 What counted were right answers on exams.

4.1 She looked up now.
4.2 She saw her instructor move down the aisle.
4.3 Her movements were smooth.
4.4 Her suit jacket was off.
4.5 Her sleeves were rolled up.

5.1 Kathy swallowed the dryness in her mouth.
5.2 The dryness was unnatural.
5.3 She glanced back at the exam.
5.4 Its words swam before her eyes.
5.5 Their swimming was dizzy.

6.1 A buzzer sounded down the hall.
6.2 The buzzer was a ten-minute warning.
6.3 She felt her insides tremble.
6.4 Her paper was still blank.

7.1 She had attended every class.
7.2 She had taken notes.
7.3 The notes were meticulous.
7.4 She had done all the assignments.
7.5 She had reviewed for the exam.
7.6 Her review was thorough.

8.1 But the exam's directions had baffled her.
8.2 The directions were unusually demanding.
8.3 "Ask a significant question about sociology."
8.4 "Answer it with what you have learned."

Writing Tip   In clusters 3 and 8, try using a colon.

Invitation   Using this paragraph as your opener, develop your case either for or against such open-ended testing in colleges.

⊃ *First Settlers*

According to the 1990 census, there were 20.1 million Hispanic-Americans in the United States, most of whom were Mexican-Americans.

1.1 History books emphasize English settlements.
1.2 The settlements were at Jamestown in 1607.
1.3 The settlements were at Plymouth in 1620.
1.4 These were part of a major immigration pattern.

2.1 But such emphasis may overlook a basic fact.
2.2 Three generations of Mexicans had put down roots.
2.3 Their roots were in the desert southwest.
2.4 The English were still anchoring their ships.

3.1 America was still far from being a republic.
3.2 A rich culture had been created by Mexicans.
3.3 They were the descendants of Toltecs.
3.4 They were the descendants of Aztecs.
3.5 They were the descendants of Mayans.
3.6 They were the descendants of Spanish soldiers.

4.1   Mexicans were like the American Indian tribes.
4.2   Mexicans welcomed Anglo visitations at first.
4.3   Mexicans later came to regret their decision.
4.4   Anglo intentions became increasingly clear.

5.1   The Mexican-American War ended in 1848.
5.2   Mexicans found themselves second-class citizens.
5.3   They lived in a foreign land.
5.4   The foreign land had once belonged to them.

6.1   The United States paid $15 million.
6.2   It received California in exchange.
6.3   It received Texas in exchange.
6.4   It received Colorado in exchange.
6.5   It received Arizona in exchange.
6.6   It received parts of Utah in exchange.
6.7   It received parts of Nevada in exchange.

7.1   Many Mexican-Americans lost land.
7.2   Their families had owned the land for centuries.
7.3   They did not understand the tax system.
7.4   They failed to file title claims.

8.1   Others were cheated by deed keepers.
8.2   The deed keepers were unscrupulous.
8.3   The deed keepers stole titles.
8.4   The deed keepers failed to record them.

Writing Tip   Try a dash + *that* as you combine cluster 2. Use series punctuation in clusters 3 and 6. For sentence variety, try opening cluster 4 with *like*.

Invitation   How important is it for "white" America to know the history of Mexican-Americans? Make your case in follow-up writing.

➲ *Motorcycle Pack*

For many of us, motorcycles hold special appeal. They suggest a life of freedom—maybe even danger—out on the open road. Listen.

1.1 We could hear them coming.
1.2 They were way off in the distance.
1.3 They were winding down the road.
1.4 The road was through the mountains.
1.5 The road was east of town.

2.1 The sound made us think of power saws.
2.2 It was deeper.
2.3 It was louder.
2.4 It was more sustained.

3.1 The first rider broke into view.
3.2 He was at the edge of town.
3.3 The brush is thick there.
3.4 The brush is full of shadows there.

4.1 The others rapped their pipes.
4.2 The others swarmed behind him.
4.3 The others brought a wave of noise.
4.4 The noise rumbled.

5.1 The leader geared down at the grocery store.
5.2 The leader set a pace.
5.3 The pace was swaggering.
5.4 The pace was through the middle of town.
5.5 He did not glance to the side.
5.6 He did not acknowledge the people.
5.7 The people watched from the sidewalk.

6.1 He personified seriousness.
6.2 He personified bravado.
6.3 His seriousness was leather.
6.4 His bravado was chrome.

7.1   The others stared at his back.
7.2   The others tried their best to imitate him.

8.1   He lifted a fist.
8.2   The fist was gloved in black.
8.3   This happened at the state highway.
8.4   The highway intersects Main Street.

9.1   The pack leaned to the right.
9.2   The pack followed his lead.
9.3   It accelerated toward the open road.
9.4   It accelerated toward a horizon.
9.5   The horizon was in the distance.

10.1   Exhaust ripped the air.
10.2   The exhaust was from the motorcycles.
10.3   The exhaust was like an insult.
10.4   It took all day to heal.

Writing Tip   Try using (but not overusing) phrases like *rapping their pipes*. See "Variety in Sentences" in Appendix B, page 224–227.

Invitation   Using "Motorcycle Pack" as a model, narrate a *brief* dramatic incident where you were an observer, taking in the scene.

⊃ *Means to Meaning*

You may think of writing as communication. But many writers see what they do as a path, one that leads from the inside out.

1.1   Writing seems simple in theory.
1.2   A person has something to say.
1.3   A person puts down a series of sentences.
1.4   The sentences are like beads on a string.

2.1   But observation of writers reveals something.
2.2   The observation is close.

2.3 The writers are skilled.
2.4 Things are often more complex than simple.

3.1 Straight lines may connect points in geometry.
3.2 Writers often work in zigzag fashion.
3.3 They follow an internal logic.
3.4 The logic is based on hunches.
3.5 The logic is based on discoveries.

4.1 Their craft is frequently messy.
4.2 Their craft is usually unpredictable.
4.3 Their craft is rarely preplanned in detail.

5.1 They typically regard writing as a process.
5.2 The process is for uncovering meanings.
5.3 The process is for inventing meanings.
5.4 The process is for clarifying meanings.
5.5 The process is not just for expressing them.

6.1 They know one thing from experience.
6.2 Words do more than dress up ideas.
6.3 Words do more than serve as a vehicle.

7.1 Words enable them to think with depth.
7.2 Words enable them to think with precision.
7.3 The words are put on paper.
7.4 The words are carefully revised.

8.1 Writing is often like a path.
8.2 The path is a means to meaning.
8.3 It helps writers educate themselves.
8.4 It helps writers nourish their spirits.

Writing Tip Try using colons and dashes in clusters 1 and 6 to see which punctuation mark is more effective.

Invitation According to this paragraph, writing is like a path. In your own writing, describe in some detail how writing is like *one* of the following: fire, ice, a bridge, an arrow, a guitar.

ↄ *Cultural Diversity*

Many literature anthologies today reflect a commitment to ethnic and cultural diversity. What rationale supports this trend?

1.1 America has always been a dynamic country.
1.2 It draws strength from its diversity.
1.3 Diversity is a mix of ethnic types.

2.1 This fact is increasingly obvious.
2.2 Population demographics have changed.
2.3 Minorities have asserted their voices.
2.4 Their voices are distinctive.

3.1 Americans value the dignity of individuals.
3.2 Americans value the worth of individuals.
3.3 Our school programs should include literature.
3.4 The literature reflects many cultures.

4.1 We celebrate our diversity.
4.2 We also acknowledge commonalities.

5.1 Hispanic voices reflect a culture.
5.2 The culture is highly integrated.
5.3 The culture is rich in traditions.
5.4 The culture looks toward the future.

6.1 Black literature offers much to readers.
6.2 It is often a literature of eloquence.
6.3 The eloquence is passionate.
6.4 It is often a literature of struggle.

7.1 Native Americans have much to teach us.
7.2 Their perspective urges us to remember history.
7.3 It urges us to protect the environment.
7.4 It urges us to seek spiritual meanings.

8.1 And Asian-Americans often address ethical issues.

8.2 Asian-Americans sometimes straddle two worlds.
8.3 They define themselves culturally.
8.4 They define themselves politically.

Writing Tip In clusters 1 and 6, try redefining the key words (*diversity* and *literature*) with follow-up phrases.

Invitation Should colleges require students to read the literary contributions of groups other than their own? Why or why not?

⊃ *Book Review*

African-American writer Ralph Ellison is one of the giants of American literature. Here's the beginning of a book review.

1.1 *Invisible Man* is Ralph Ellison's novel.
1.2 The novel is brilliantly written.
1.3 It records a journey from innocence.
1.4 It records a journey to experience.
1.5 The journey is painful.

2.1 In it a hero becomes aware of his color.
2.2 The hero is African-American.
2.3 A hero learns of his invisibility to whites.
2.4 The whites control his life.

3.1 This awareness occurs gradually.
3.2 It occurs through seven episodes.
3.3 The episodes are confrontations.
3.4 The confrontations are violent.

4.1 The first is the "Battle Royal."
4.2 The Battle Royal is a boxing match.
4.3 The match is staged to entertain whites.
4.4 The whites are sadistic.

5.1 The hero is blindfolded.
5.2 He is forced to fight with other blacks.
5.3 The blacks are his friends.
5.4 They have also been blindfolded.

6.1 He is goaded by fear.
6.2 He is goaded by taunts from the crowd.
6.3 He is goaded by his own pain.
6.4 He lashes out at his opponents.
6.5 His opponents hit back in response.

7.1 His humanity is denied by whites.
7.2 The hero becomes an animal.
7.3 The animal is cornered.
7.4 The animal is fighting for its life.

8.1 His victory gift is a briefcase.
8.2 The gift is ironic.
8.3 The briefcase symbolizes his education.
8.4 It marks the beginning of his self-awareness.

Writing Tip For sentence variety, try opening cluster 6 with *goaded*. See "Variety in Sentences" in Appendix B, pages 224-227.

Invitation This review, while incomplete, shows one approach to discussing literature. Begin your own review of a poem, story, book, or movie. Focus on what the hero or heroine *learns*.

⊃ Chicano Literature

Have you read literature produced by Mexican-Americans? Here's an overview of creative work you might like to look into.

1.1 Chicano authors produce poetry.
1.2 The poetry is superb.
1.3 They produce novels.
1.4 The novels are exciting.
1.5 They produce short stories.
1.6 The short stories are engaging.

2.1 Gary Soto has written wonderful books.
2.2 He is a Chicano poet.
2.3 He is well known for clear writing.
2.4 His writing deals with everyday life.
2.5 One of the books is titled *Black Hair*.

3.1   Sandra Cisneros achieved recognition.
3.2   Her recognition was widespread.
3.3   She published *The House on Mango Street.*
3.4   This presents forty-four vignettes.
3.5   The vignettes are keenly observed.
3.6   These are from a feminine perspective.

4.1   Another popular novelist is Rudolfo Anaya.
4.2   He has written several Chicano books.
4.3   The books include *Bless Me, Ultima.*
4.4   It won the Premio Quinto Sol in 1971.
4.5   The books include *The Heart of Aztlan.*

5.1   Anaya also wrote *The Silence of Llano.*
5.2   This is a fine collection of stories.
5.3   The stories have varied settings.
5.4   Many high school readers will enjoy them.

6.1   Chicano literature is so rich.
6.2   Chicano literature is so varied.
6.3   You may want to consult your librarian.
6.4   You may want to consult *Chicano Literature.*
6.5   This is a reference book by Charles Tatum.

Writing Tip   In clusters 2, 5, and 6, practice making appositives—phrases that describe the nouns they follow.

Invitation   Using this paragraph as a model, introduce readers to *another* type of literature—that of black Americans, Native Americans, Asian-Americans, or some other group.

⊃ *Big Ada*

Sometimes an unforgettable character touches your life and changes it. Have you known a person like that?

1.1   Every town has drifters.
1.2   The drifters come and go.
1.3   They rarely affect people's lives.
1.4   Such was not the case with Big Ada.

2.1   She was the town's local character.
2.2   She lived in an apartment over a tavern.
2.3   She sang old folk songs for meals there.
2.4   She strummed her guitar for meals there.

3.1   People called her a "free spirit."
3.2   No one knew her real name.
3.3   No one knew her age.
3.4   No one new anything about her.

4.1   Her apparel was practical.
4.2   Her apparel was unconventional.
4.3   She wore a fringed leather jacket.
4.4   She wore a cowboy hat with a high crown.
4.5   She wore well-faded denim jeans.
4.6   She wore pointed boots.

5.1   And her routine was always the same.
5.2   Her routine was in the afternoons.
5.3   She roamed the town on foot.
5.4   She ended up in front of the drugstore.
5.5   She talked to neighborhood children there.
5.6   She listened to their adventures.

6.1   There she sang their requests.
6.2   She told them stories.
6.3   The stores were richly detailed.
6.4   She helped them sort out their troubles.
6.5   Their troubles were momentary.

7.1   Ada was warm and jocular.
7.2   Ada was a natural teacher.
7.3   Then she left without a trace.
7.4   No one knew why.

8.1   The sheriff found only one clue.
8.2   It was in a trash basket in Ada's room.
8.3   It was a scrap of napkin.
8.4   The napkin was crumpled.

9.1   On it was drawn a lone figure.
9.2   The figure seemed trapped in a cage.
9.3   The cage was boxlike.
9.4   The cage had bars.

10.1   People wondered about this.
10.2   What did the box symbolize?
10.3   What did the bars symbolize.
10.4   What did the figure symbolize?
10.5   Their questions remain unanswered.

Writing Tip In cluster 4, check your punctuation of items in a series.

Invitation Big Ada was—and perhaps still is—a real person. What might she have secretly written about her reasons for leaving?

⊃ *Moral Dilemma*

Moral dilemmas surround us—in sexual relationships and at tax time, for example. But what about the dilemma the soldier faces?

1.1 A dilemma is a problem.
1.2 The problem has two solutions.
1.3 Both solutions have consequences.
1.4 The consequences are negative.

2.1 The Nuremberg war trials followed World War II.
2.2 The trials posed a dilemma for individuals.
2.3 The individuals were thoughtful.
2.4 The individuals were all over the world.

3.1 The trials judged Nazi officers.
3.2 The officers participated in mass executions.
3.3 Six million Jews were executed.
3.4 The Jews were in German concentration camps.

4.1 The prosecution argued this.
4.2 The officers were guilty of crimes.
4.3 The crimes were against humanity.
4.4 The officers had a moral responsibility.
4.5 The responsibility was to the human race.

5.1 The defense argued this.
5.2 The officers were not personally responsible.
5.3 They were carrying out military orders.
5.4 The orders were from Hitler's high command.

6.1   Many officers were found guilty of war crimes.
6.2   They were sentenced to death or imprisonment.
6.3   Nuremberg raised basic moral questions.
6.4   All soldiers must face these questions today.

7.1   Should individuals disobey orders?
7.2   The individuals are in the military.
7.3   The individuals thereby risk punishment.
7.4   The punishment is from superiors.
7.5   Should individuals follow orders?
7.6   The orders conflict with personal values.

8.1   Let's consider this dilemma more carefully.
8.2   The dilemma is stark and simple.
8.3   This is to provide one person's response.

Writing Tip   Try opening cluster 6 with *because* as a connecting word. This subordinator applies to sentences 6.1 and 6.2.

Invitation   War legalizes killing. But under what circumstances, in your view, would a soldier be morally justified in disobeying the orders of superior officers? Continue the discussion.

⊃ *Crucial Pass*

Games are sometimes decided in the last few seconds—with one play left. What's the most exciting sports event you ever witnessed?

1.1   The quarterback glanced left and right.
1.2   The quarterback barked sharp signals.
1.3   The quarterback took the snap.
1.4   The quarterback dropped straight back.
1.5   The ball was tucked against his thigh.

2.1 He wheeled to the right.
2.2 He feinted a handoff to the halfback.
2.3 The halfback was slanting off tackle.
2.4 He then circled into a pocket of blockers.
2.5 The pocket was protective.

3.1 The halfback crashed into the line.
3.2 His body was crouched.
3.3 His knees were churning and lifting.
3.4 The quarterback glanced downfield.
3.5 He felt his fingers tighten on the football.

4.1 The tight end had come across the line.
4.2 He had headed for the defensive linebacker.
4.3 The linebacker was burly.
4.4 The linebacker was dropping back.
4.5 His hands were up.

5.1 The end had faked to the outside.
5.2 The end had slowed down dramatically.
5.3 The end had taken a backward glance.
5.4 Then he had spurted suddenly up the middle.
5.5 He had left the defender behind.

6.1 The quarterback pumped the ball twice.
6.2 The quarterback watched the downfield action.
6.3 The end changed pace.
6.4 The end broke into the clear.

7.1 Now the end was in the open.
7.2 He was angling toward the goal line.
7.3 The football was lofting into a blue sky.
7.4 It was a perfectly thrown spiral.
7.5 He would catch it on a dead run.

8.1 The end's fingers were outstretched.
8.2 The end followed the ball's trajectory.
8.3 The trajectory was descending.

8.4 The end gathered it in with a leap.
8.5 The end headed for a homecoming victory.
8.6 The victory was never to be forgotten.

Writing Tip To make absolute phrases, delete *was* and *were* in sentences 3.2 and 3.3. Then combine.

Invitation Describe what happened at the victory celebration. Or write about a memorable victory (or loss) you have known.

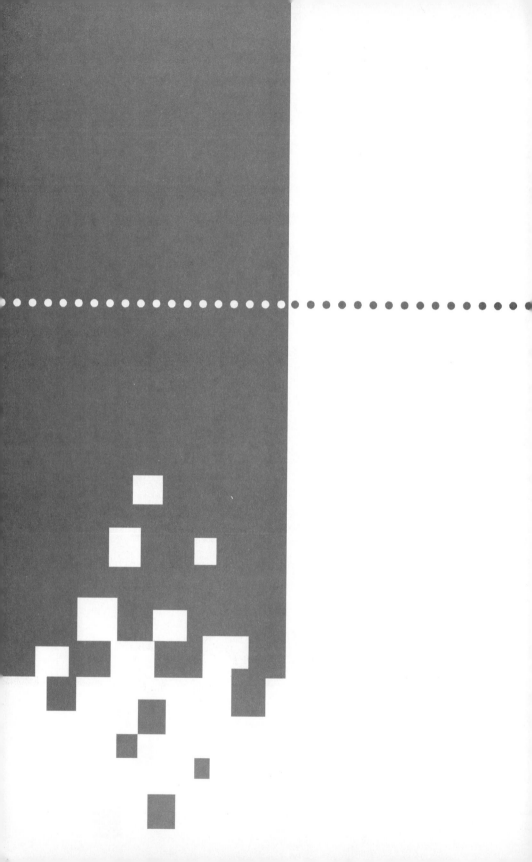

Advanced Combining

Say the word *writing,* and most of us picture black squiggles of print on a white background. What matters to us is an orderly sequence of sentences marching left to right and down the page. We rarely think about the *white space* that surrounds sentences. After all, why is that important?

But imagine, for a moment, the existence of space-absorbing aliens that have just erased all the white space in the textbooks you've worked so hard to buy. What you would face, of course, are sentences run together in solid black rectangles of text—page after page, without paragraph breaks or headings. Under such unhappy circumstances, studying could become a *real* chore.

In this unit of advanced combining, we focus on *paragraphs*—what they are, why they're important, and how you can write them more successfully. You can learn more about this topic by reading Appendix B, "Sentence and Paragraph Strategies," which contains more information on paragraph organization and packaging (page 221).

A PACKAGE FOR SENTENCES

Let's think for a moment about paragraphs, just to remind ourselves what they are and how they work. As you look at the paragraphs on this page, for example, you see that indention—a bit of white space—introduces each set of sentences. Why? Because readers need visual rests from time to time. Paragraphs break up the flow of writing just as pauses break up the flow of speech.

Equally important, however, paragraphs help a writer shift to a different voice (for example, in dialogue) or to a new idea. Each paragraph provides a way of grouping (or clustering) related sentences. Therefore, you might think of each paragraph as a "chunk" of meaning—a visual "package" for sentences. It is by skillfully grouping (or packaging) sentences that writers organize and advance what they want to say.

To further understand these points, you might think of paragraphs as plastic packaging wrap—the see-through stuff for food storage. Imagine, for a moment, that you want to *organize* leftover meats and cheeses in the bottom section of your old refrigerator after a party. You'd probably begin by putting meats and cheeses in different packages. After all, it's hard to imagine any logical reason for putting slices of turkey, beef, and ham in the same package with slices of cheddar, gouda, and Swiss cheese.

In our imaginary refrigerator, if you had just a few slices of meat, you'd probably package them together; however, if you had several slices of each kind, they'd probably go in different packages. The same logic applies to the different cheeses. If you had one or two slices of each, you might put them in the same package, just for convenience. But if you had several of each, you'd probably package them into separate groups. The whole point of packaging is to work with what's on hand and make it easily accessible.

By analogy, the principles described above also work with paragraphing. In other words, paragraphs *organize* writing by packaging sentences into logical, easily accessible groups. These visual chunks of meaning can be sequenced, rearranged, split apart, or combined. Simply put, there's no set definition or "form" for paragraphs. Some paragraphs are short, others long; some are loosely organized, others highly structured.

However, a paragraph is more than a random collection of sentences. The sentences in a paragraph usually have a common purpose—for example, to describe a place, narrate an action, explain an idea, or argue an opinion. Of course, the *longer* the description, narration, explanation, or argument, the more that paragraphing will come into play. The key to successful paragraphing, when all is said and done, is your ability to see what goes with what and to put yourself in the reader's shoes, reading with his or her eyes, as well as your own.

DEVELOPING PARAGRAPH SKILLS

Exercises in Unit 3 develop your ability to make paragraphs and to organize them into effective sequences. Each SC exercise is composed of two separate (but related) paragraphs on the same topic. By combining sentences as usual, you'll construct two paragraphs in a larger composition. You may work either on your own or with others as you do the sentence combining.

After constructing paragraphs from the given sentences, you can begin creating paragraphs of your own. Your basic task is to tie everything together into an interesting multiparagraph paper. Read the Invitation that follows each half of the total SC exercise; this will give you general direction for follow-up writing of your own. You may wish to swap ideas with workshop partners before you begin writing.

Creating paragraphs in this way stimulates your thinking and also helps you solve basic problems in sequencing and organization. Instead of facing all the tasks of writing at once, you can *focus* your energies—taking time, for example, to compare your paragraphs with those written by your workshop partners. Also, advanced work in combining helps you think *strategically* about writing.

What is a *strategic approach?* Thinking strategically means worrying less about individual sentences and more about paragraphs. It is paragraphs, after all, that provide a reader with "chunks" of meaning. Put another way, a strategic writing approach, like an aerial view, helps you see and understand the Big Picture. When you're concerned only about individual sentences—and therefore *not* thinking strategically—you can find yourself stuck with a ground-level perspective, one that limits your horizons.

It's important to understand here that you may alter the content of SC paragraphs or rearrange them to suit your emerging purposes. This is advanced combining, so anything goes. Try to think *strategically* as you create generalizations, link paragraphs together, or develop examples to support a position. Ask yourself: *What would make sense here? How can I accomplish this? Where will this take the reader?*

Remember to check Appendix B (page 221) for additional ideas on paragraph organization and paragraph packaging.

⊃ *Classroom Crisis*

Directions   Combine sentences to create the *first* of four paragraphs. Then work on the Invitation below for the *second* paragraph. "School Reform" follows this exercise.

1.1   The United States has long been a world leader.
1.2   This is because of its education system.
1.3   Standards now appear to be slipping.

2.1   Teachers call for homework.
2.2   The teachers are frustrated.
2.3   Many students simply shrug.
2.4   Many students make up excuses.

3.1   This scene is increasingly common.
3.2   It occurs in American high schools.
3.3   They once stood as symbols of excellence.

4.1   Many American students don't work very hard.
4.2   The students are in high school.

4.3 This is according to researchers.
4.4 They have studied homework patterns.

5.1 Only 26 percent study from one to two hours.
5.2 Only 12 percent study over two hours.
5.3 These percentages are per night.

6.1 Two-thirds study for less than an hour.
6.2 This is each night.
6.3 Many do not study at all.

7.1 U.S. students do get high marks in one activity.
7.2 The high marks are consistent.
7.3 The activity occurs after school.

8.1 They watch TV three or four hours each day.
8.2 They spend 15,000 hours in front of the tube.
8.3 This is from grade 1 through grade 12.
8.4 This compares with 13,000 hours in school.

9.1 Critics of education contend something.
9.2 Students elsewhere develop their minds.
9.3 Many American kids let theirs turn to mush.

Writing Tip For clusters 1 and 9, try several connectors—*but, yet, however, while, although*—before settling on one. Check your punctuation.

Invitation Use your own observations to explain—from an insider's point of view—why many American high school students neglect their academic homework.

⊃ *School Reform*

Directions "Classroom Crisis" precedes this exercise. Combine sentences to create the *third* of four paragraphs. Then work on the Invitation below for the *fourth* paragraph.

1.1 Knowledge is the key to survival.
1.2 The world becomes a global village.
1.3 The village is interdependent.

2.1 Mediocrity threatens our future security.
2.2 Mediocrity threatens our economic position.
2.3 The mediocrity is in educational standards.
2.4 It reduces our competitiveness.

3.1 There are many ways to raise standards.
3.2 The standards are for high school students.
3.3 One possible approach is to establish tests.
3.4 The tests are for college admission.

4.1 This approach works in many other countries.
4.2 The countries include Japan.
4.3 The countries include Germany.
4.4 They are noted for educational excellence.

5.1 Our present college system has its good points.
5.2 The system emphasizes "open admissions."
5.3 Many students don't take it seriously.
5.4 They simply glide through high school.

6.1 They face college-level work.
6.2 They are often rudely awakened.
6.3 They do not possess the requisite knowledge.
6.4 They do not possess the requisite skills.
6.5 They are forced to drop out.

7.1 Dreams crumble quickly.
7.2 They are not built on firm foundations.

8.1 Such tests will not solve school problems.
8.2 They may encourage students to study harder.
8.3 They may help prepare America for the future.

Writing Tip   In cluster 5, try *however* as a connector; this connector should be preceded by a semicolon (;) and followed by a comma.

Invitation   Write about a second possible approach to school reform that addresses the "Classroom Crisis." Share your text with a writing partner, and use his or her feedback to revise.

⊃ *Black Music*

Directions   Combine sentences to create the *second* of four paragraphs. Then work on the Invitation below for the *first* paragraph. "Copycats" follows this exercise.

1.1   Music has been shaped by black musicians.
1.2   The music is in the twentieth century.
1.3   The shaping has been irrevocable.

2.1   Ragtime became popular 100 years ago.
2.2   The blues became popular 100 years ago.
2.3   This was thanks to Afro-Americans.
2.4   They defined these new sounds.
2.5   They refined these new sounds.

3.1   Improvisation subsequently led to jazz.
3.2   Historians now view jazz as an expression.
3.3   The expression was uniquely American.
3.4   Jazz was a form developed by blacks.

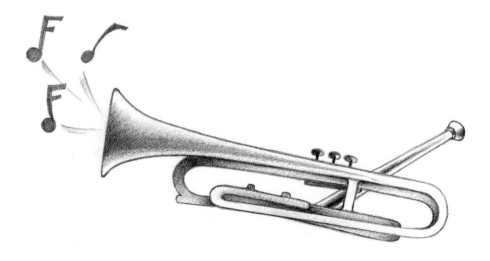

4.1 Then came rhythm and blues.
4.2 Rhythm and blues was during the 1940s.
4.3 Then came rock and roll.
4.4 Rock and roll was during the 1950s.
4.5 Then came soul music.
4.6 Soul music was during the 1960s.

5.1 The 1970s saw further expressions.
5.2 The 1980s saw further expressions.
5.3 The expressions were Afro-American.
5.4 The expressions included funky disco.
5.5 The expressions included reggae.
5.6 The expressions included rap music.

6.1 Each form had its musical roots.
6.2 The roots were in black communities.

7.1 Afro-Americans invented these sounds.
7.2 White musicians quickly copied them.
7.3 White musicians exploited their potential.
7.4 The potential was commercial.

Writing Tip To make an appositive—a renaming phrase like this—focus on cluster 3, sentence 3.4.

Invitation Develop a vivid character sketch of your favorite black musician—in action—to introduce "Black Music."

⊃ *Copycats*

Directions "Black Music" precedes this exercise. Combine sentences to create the *third* of four paragraphs. Then work on the Invitation below for the *fourth* paragraph.

1.1   Copycats included Elvis Presley.
1.2   Copycats included the Beatles.
1.3   Copycats included the Rolling Stones.
1.4   The copycats were prominent.
1.5   All of them enjoyed great success.

2.1   Today's imitators are a diverse group.
2.2   The group includes Vanilla Ice.
2.3   The group includes New Kids on the Block.
2.4   The group includes Mariah Carey.
2.5   The group includes Michael Bolton.

3.1   Rap music clearly illustrates something.
3.2   Rap music is a form of street poetry.
3.3   It was born in urban ghettos during the 1980s.
3.4   "Imitation is the highest form of flattery."

4.1   M.C. Hammer popularized rap.
4.2   L.L. Cool J popularized rap.
4.3   Heavy D popularized rap.
4.4   Vanilla Ice imitated the new sound.
4.5   Vanilla Ice put it at the top of pop charts.

5.1   Vanilla Ice even adopted a black haircut.
5.2   Vanilla Ice even adopted lined eyebrows.
5.3   These were to complement Running Man moves.
5.4   The moves were borrowed from Hammer's shows.

6.1   Such imitations of black music will continue.
6.2   Few can copy Michael Jackson's "Moonwalk."
6.3   Few can copy Janet Jackson's performances.
6.4   The performances are inimitable.

7.1   And fans accept no substitutes for Prince.
7.2   Fans accept no substitutes for Whitney Houston.
7.3   They are in a class by themselves.

Writing Tip   In clusters 4 and 6, try several connectors—*but, yet, however, while, although*—before deciding on one.

Invitation Write a conclusion for "Black Music" and "Copy-cats" to explain *why* such borrowing may have occurred. Share your text with a writing partner, and use his or her feedback to revise.

⊃ *A Right to Die*

Directions Combine sentences to create the *second* of four paragraphs. Then work on the Invitation below for the *first* paragraph. "Final Rights" follows this exercise.

1.1 Our Constitution guarantees certain rights.
1.2 The rights are inalienable.
1.3 It does not guarantee "the right to die."

2.1 Doctors take the Hippocratic oath.
2.2 The oath obliges them to sustain life.
2.3 The oath obliges them to eschew mercy killing.

3.1 Hospitals sometimes demean patients.
3.2 The patients are terminally ill.
3.3 The patients want to die with dignity.
3.4 The hospitals hook up life-support systems.
3.5 The hospitals administer unwanted drugs.

4.1 These three facts cause concern.
4.2 The concern is among many Americans.
4.3 The Americans want to exercise choice.
4.4 The choice is in how they live.
4.5 The choice is in how they die.

5.1 Technology may produce unwanted outcomes.
5.2 "Living wills" are increasingly popular.
5.3 "Living wills" specify personal decisions.
5.4 The decisions are for terminal health care.

6.1 Changing values are also seen in surveys.
6.2 The values are American.
6.3 The values concern "the right to die."
6.4 The surveys sample public opinion.

7.1 Many Americans see suicide as an option.
7.2 The percentage is two-thirds, to be exact.
7.3 The option is defensible.
7.4 The option is for patients.
7.5 They have "no hope for improvement."
7.6 This is according to a 1990 Gallup poll.

Writing Tip   In cluster 5, try *because* as a sentence opener, and use *that* with sentence 5.3. In cluster 7, try a pair of dashes with sentence 7.2

Invitation   To introduce "A Right to Die" and "Final Rights," develop a paragraph that describes a terminally ill patient in a hospital setting.

⊃ *Final Rights*

Directions "A Right to Die" precedes this exercise. Combine sentences to create the *third* of four paragraphs. Then work on the Invitation below for the *fourth* paragraph.

1.1 Dying has become a complex issue.
1.2 Dying is a basic fact of life.
1.3 The issue is in America.
1.4 This is thanks to advanced technology.

2.1 Medical science can now sustain life.
2.2 The sustenance is for months or years.
2.3 Many families face ethical questions.
2.4 The questions are profound.
2.5 They concern life-support systems.

3.1 Family members often see loved ones.
3.2 The loved ones have no hope of recovery.
3.3 The loved ones linger on in hospitals.
3.4 The loved ones linger on in nursing homes.

4.1 Sometimes they are in pain.
4.2 Sometimes they are unconscious.
4.3 They are usually kept alive by machines.
4.4 The machines are sophisticated.
4.5 The machines are expensive.

5.1 Quality of life is often absent.
5.2 The loved one hovers in limbo.
5.3 The limbo is between life and death.
5.4 Family members watch helplessly.

6.1 Machines can soon drain life savings.
6.2 The machines are whirring.
6.3 The machines keep a loved one alive.
6.4 This leaves a bleak financial future.
6.5 The future is for family members.

7.1   High technology may sustain life.
7.2   It also prolongs the process of dying.
7.3   Many people now find this objectionable.

Writing Tip   For sentence variety, try deleting *they are* in sentences 4.1 and 4.2. In cluster 7, try *while* or *although* as a sentence opener.

Invitation   Draw conclusions that assert your personal values on this profoundly human issue. Share your text with a writing partner, and use his or her feedback to revise.

Ɔ Smoking Facts

Directions   Combine sentences to create the *second* of four paragraphs. Then work on the Invitation below for the *first* paragraph. "More Smoking Facts" follows this exercise.

1.1   The evidence is undeniable.
1.2   The evidence is scientific.
1.3   Smoking promotes heart disease.
1.4   Smoking promotes cancer.

2.1   Smoking leads to premature deaths.
2.2   The deaths are preventable.
2.3   The deaths are for 350,000 Americans.
2.4   The deaths occur each year.

3.1   Major risks include cancer of the lungs.
3.2   They include cancer of the throat.
3.3   They include cancer of the mouth.
3.4   Cancer of the esophagus is also a threat.
3.5   Bladder cancer is also a threat.

4.1 Lung cancer is particularly deadly.
4.2 It is a disease of smokers.
4.3 It kills 90 percent of its victims.

5.1 Smoking also causes heart disease.
5.2 It damages the lining of the arteries.
5.3 It raises blood pressure.
5.4 It contributes to atherosclerosis.
5.5 Atherosclerosis impedes blood flow.

6.1 Heart attacks kill 200,000 smokers.
6.2 This is each year in the United States.
6.3 Many smokers refuse to kick their habit.
6.4 This is even after a heart attack.

7.1 Most smokers are aware of the danger.
7.2 Most smokers are addicted to nicotine.
7.3 Nicotine is a powerful drug.
7.4 The drug stimulates the nervous system.
7.5 Most smokers choose to deny the risks.

Writing Tip   In clusters 4 and 7, try inserting an appositive—a short renaming phrase like this—into the base sentence.

Invitation   Develop a character sketch or dramatic incident to introduce "Smoking Facts" and "More Smoking Facts."

⊃ *More Smoking Facts*

Directions   "Smoking Facts" precedes this exercise. Combine sentences to create the *third* of four paragraphs. Then work on the Invitation below for the *fourth* paragraph.

1.1   Each day 3000 Americans take up smoking.
1.2   The Americans are mostly teenagers.
1.3   They have heard of its health effects.
1.4   The effects are adverse.

2.1   Adolescents may smoke to gain peer approval.
2.2   They may smoke to express rebelliousness.
2.3   They may smoke simply out of curiosity.

3.1   Modeling is often a major factor.
3.2   Modeling is the emulation of others' behavior.
3.3   The factor contributes to a decision to smoke.

4.1   Young men may choose Marlboro cigarettes.
4.2   They fantasize themselves as rugged.
4.3   They fantasize themselves as handsome.
4.4   This is like the first Marlboro Man.
4.5   The first Marlboro Man died of emphysema.

5.1   Young women may choose Virginia Slims.
5.2   They want to appear good-looking.
5.3   They want to appear sophisticated.
5.4   They want to appear "with-it."
5.5   There is nothing sexy about lung cancer.

6.1   Advertisers work hard to create images.
6.2   The images appeal to teenagers.
6.3   Adolescents are defining their identities.
6.4   Adolescents are defining their life-styles.

7.1   Smokers are shown having lots of fun.
7.2   They look beautiful in the process.

8.1   These images work on teenagers' minds.
8.2   These images team up with social factors.
8.3   The result is one million new smokers annually.

Writing Tip To emphasize parallelism, consider using dashes with sentences 4.4 and 5.5. See "Parallelism in Sentences" in Appendix B, pages 221–224.

Invitation Write a concluding paragraph for "Smoking Facts" and "More Smoking Facts." Share your text with a writing partner, and use his or her feedback to revise.

⊃ *Hypnotic Trance*

Directions Combine sentences to create the *first* of four paragraphs. Then work on the Invitation below for the *second* paragraph. "Hypnosis Applications" follows this exercise.

1.1 Hypnosis is a condition.
1.2 The condition is trancelike.
1.3 It is usually induced by suggestions.
1.4 The suggestions are verbal.

2.1 Hypnotists employ various techniques.
2.2 These may involve focusing on a voice.
2.3 These may involve focusing on an object.
2.4 These may involve focusing on a mental image.

3.1 Hypnotized subjects appear to be awake.
3.2 They soon enter another state of being.
3.3 The state of being is much like sleep.
3.4 They become responsive to instructions.

4.1 Suggestions work on the subconscious mind.
4.2 The suggestions are subsequent.
4.3 They bypass conscious awareness.

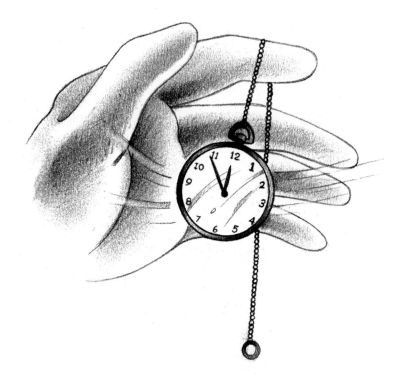

4.4 This is particularly for motivated subjects.
4.5 The subjects are readily hypnotized.

5.1 Verbal cues can anesthetize the body.
5.2 Hypnotized subjects do not experience pain.

6.1 Subjects can alter heart rate.
6.2 Subjects can alter respiration.
6.3 Subjects can alter stomach acid secretion.
6.4 Subjects can turn on their immune systems.

7.1 Age regression can be induced.
7.2 Hypnotized subjects experience past events.
7.3 The past events are dimly remembered.

8.1 And cancer patients can undergo chemotherapy.
8.2 The cancer patients have been hypnotized.
8.3 This is without suffering nausea.

Writing Tip In cluster 3, try *although* as a sentence opener; then try a semicolon + *however* to join sentences. Which do you prefer?

Invitation Write about a life experience that you would like to relive through hypnosis. What details can you presently remember about this event? Why would you like to relive it?

⊃ *Hypnosis Applications*

Directions "Hypnotic Trance" precedes this exercise. Combine sentences to create the *third* of four paragraphs. Then work on the Invitation below for the *fourth* paragraph.

1.1 Hypnosis has many positive benefits.
1.2 Hypnosis does not cure disease.
1.3 Hypnotists do not have magical powers.

2.1 Dentists sometimes hypnotize patients.
2.2 This makes a painkiller unnecessary.
2.3 Some surgeons use hypnotic suggestions.
2.4 The suggestions are after operations.
2.5 Their purpose is to reduce bleeding.

3.1 Hypnosis can reduce pain for burn patients.
3.2 Hypnosis can speed recovery for burn patients.
3.3 They get treatment soon after their injury.

4.1 Psychiatrists can use hypnosis as therapy.
4.2 They first help patients explore events.
4.3 The events have been traumatic.
4.4 The events have been repressed.
4.5 They then help them deal with emotions.
4.6 The emotions are triggered by the events.

5.1 Hypnosis has many applications in medicine.
5.2 Its benefits are not limited to that field.

6.1   Police officers investigate crimes.
6.2   They sometimes use hypnosis as a tool.
6.3   The tool helps witnesses remember facts.
6.4   The facts include descriptions of criminals.
6.5   The facts include license plate numbers.

7.1   And TV advertisers plan their slogans.
7.2   They plan their songs.
7.3   They plan their visual sequences.
7.4   They use principles of hypnosis.
7.5   They want heightened awareness of messages.
7.6   The messages market their products.

Writing Tip   In cluster 4, try a dash for emphasis; in clusters 6 and 7, try a connector like *when* to create parallelism. See "Parallelism in Sentences" in Appendix B, pages 221–224.

Invitation   Write about a TV advertisement whose suggestions "stick in the mind." Why do you think this ad is effective? Share your text with a writing partner, and use his or her feedback to revise.

⊃ Shoeshine Boy

Directions   Combine sentences to create the *first* of four paragraphs. Then work on the Invitation below for the *second* paragraph. "Executive Traveler" follows this exercise.

1.1   The Boy is a grown man.
1.2   The man works at the airport.
1.3   The man shines shoes six days a week.
1.4   This is all he knows as a trade.

2.1   He is Caucasian.
2.2   He might also be African-American.

2.3 He might also be Asian.
2.4 He might also be Hispanic.

3.1 He reaches for his cleaning brush.
3.2 He makes soapy circles on the leather.
3.3 He wipes its surface clean.

4.1 This preparation is complete.
4.2 He selects his wax.
4.3 He skims a film with his fingertips.
4.4 He applies it with quick strokes.
4.5 The strokes are back and forth.

5.1 His tongue darts between his teeth.
5.2 This is part of his routine.
5.3 The routine is "polished."
5.4 The routine is mindless.

6.1 He brushes the leather with open palms.
6.2 This is to work up a dull shine.
6.3 He then squeezes a rag dry.
6.4 He winds it in tight loops.
6.5 The loops are around his index finger.
6.6 This is to scoop crescents of dark wax.

7.1 The shine begins to come.
7.2 It moves up through the film.
7.3 It reflects the neon lights.
7.4 The Boy reaches for a clear wax.
7.5 This is the finishing touch.

8.1 He finally reaches for a cloth.
8.2 The cloth is soft and stained.
8.3 He flicks it over the shoes.
8.4 He whips the shine to attention.

9.1 The cloth pops between his hands.
9.2 The cloth crackles between his hands.
9.3 His hands are nervous and long-fingered.
9.4 They coax light from the leather.

Writing Tip   Consider the word *although* as an opener for cluster 2 and *when* as an opener for cluster 4.

Invitation   Write a *second* paragraph that explains how certain types of work can demean people rather than uplift them.

ↄ *Executive Traveler*

Directions   "Shoeshine Boy" precedes this exercise. Combine sentences to create the *fourth* of four paragraphs. Then work on the Invitation below for the *third* paragraph.

1.1   The Executive closes his *Wall Street Journal.*
1.2   The Executive descends from his chair.
1.3   His chair is thronelike.
1.4   He gives the Boy a nod.

2.1   He is African-American.
2.2   He might also be Caucasian.
2.3   He might also be Asian.
2.4   He might also be Hispanic.

3.1   He does not comment on the shine.
3.2   He fishes for his wallet.
3.3   The Boy waits.

4.1   Payment will be met with a stare.
4.2   The payment includes no tip.
4.3   The stare is surly and disgusted.
4.4   It is meant to be insulting.

5.1   Payment with tip will be met with a smile.
5.2   Payment with tip will be met with a wink.
5.3   Payment with tip will be met with wishes.
5.4   The wishes are for safe travel.

6.1 The Boy reaches for his change.
6.2 His reach is reluctant.
6.3 The Executive checks his watch.
6.4 The Executive heads for the airport lobby.

7.1 He moves smoothly down the hallway.
7.2 His shoes gleam beneath his stride.
7.3 His stride is confident.

8.1 The Boy turns back to his wax.
8.2 The Boy turns back to his rags.
8.3 The Boy readies himself for more shoes.

Writing Tip Try using (but not overusing) participle phrases as you combine clusters 6, 7, and 8.

Invitation Create a *third* paragraph that argues for respecting the work of others, regardless of differences in status.

⊃ Before AIDS

Directions Combine sentences to create the *first* of four paragraphs. Then work on the Invitation below for the *second* paragraph. "Black Death" follows this exercise.

1.1 People have always feared the unknown.
1.2 It is difficult to appreciate the fear.
1.3 The fear accompanied bubonic plagues.
1.4 They were during medieval times.
1.5 They were during the Renaissance.
1.6 They were during the nineteenth century.

2.1 The disease was called the Black Death.
2.2 This was during the Middle Ages.

2.3 This was because of the disease's effects.
2.4 The effects were on the human body.

3.1 Fever marked the Black Death.
3.2 Chills marked the Black Death.
3.3 Swelling marked the Black Death.
3.4 The swelling was severe.
3.5 The swelling was of the lymph nodes.

4.1 The disease was accompanied by hemorrhages.
4.2 The hemorrhages made dark spots.
4.3 The spots were on the skin.
4.4 The disease had a mortality rate.
4.5 The mortality rate was extremely high.

5.1 Hundreds of thousands died in Europe.
5.2 Hundreds of thousands died in England.
5.3 This was during the fourteenth century.

6.1 The Black Death broke out again.
6.2 This was during the seventeenth century.

6.3 Lyons lost half its population.
6.4 Milan lost 86,000 people.
6.5 The Venetian Republic lost 500,000.

7.1 The plague swept the continent.
7.2 This was during the eighteenth century.
7.3 It killed about 60,000 in Moscow.
7.4 It killed about 215,000 in Brandenburg.
7.5 It killed about 300,000 in Austria.

8.1 The last outbreak occurred in China.
8.2 This was during the nineteenth century.
8.3 The plague was then carried far and wide.
8.4 Oceangoing vessels embarked from seaports.
8.5 It finally reached San Francisco in 1902.

Writing Tip   Use a transitional expression like *similarly* or *in the same way* to introduce the second paragraph, which will deal with AIDS.

Invitation   In a comparison, show how AIDS—much like the bubonic plague of earlier centuries—has become the feared epidemic of our time.

➲ *Black Death*

Directions   "Before AIDS" precedes this exercise. Combine sentences to create the *third* of four paragraphs. Then work on the Invitation below for the *fourth* paragraph.

1.1 The Black Death had a cause.
1.2 It was not understood until 1894.
1.3 The cause was not confirmed until 1908.

2.1 Only then did people understand something.
2.2 The disease was carried by fleas.
2.3 The fleas lived on rats.
2.4 The fleas lived on other rodents.

3.1 Something is unfortunate.
3.2 The infected fleas have now spread.
3.3 The spread has been over the western United States.
3.4 The spread has even been into Canada.

4.1 Thirty-eight rodents now carry the fleas.
4.2 The rodents are wild.
4.3 They include rats.
4.4 They include squirrels.
4.5 They include prairie dogs.
4.6 They include rabbits.
4.7 They include meadow mice.

5.1 Control of rodents is exercised in areas.
5.2 The areas are susceptible to epidemics.
5.3 The susceptibility is potential.
5.4 The areas are especially the cities.

6.1 DDT was once used to control the fleas.
6.2 DDT has serious side effects.
6.3 The effects are damaging to life.
6.4 The effects are damaging to the environment.

7.1 The Black Death is still with us.
7.2 It is a legacy from the past.
7.3 It now seems less frightening.
7.4 Its cause is understood.

Writing Tip Use a transitional word or phrase to switch focus from the bubonic plague to the topic of AIDS in paragraph 4.

Invitation Write a concluding paragraph (paragraph 4) that describes the cause and spread of AIDS. Share your text with a writing partner, and use his or her feedback to revise.

⊃ *Alcohol Facts*

Directions Combine sentences to create the *second* of four paragraphs. Then work on the Invitation below for the *first* paragraph. "More Alcohol Facts" follows this exercise.

1.1 Alcohol is the most widely used drug.
1.2 It is a product of fermentation.
1.3 The product is natural.

2.1 Teenagers are curious about alcohol.
2.2 About two-thirds of them try it out.
2.3 About one-third develop problems.

3.1 Most youthful drinkers start early.
3.2 The drinkers develop addictions.
3.3 The drinkers get into trouble with police.
3.4 This is often before age thirteen.

4.1 Many are unaware of certain facts.
4.2 Alcohol can damage the brain.
4.3 Alcohol can damage the heart.
4.4 Alcohol can damage the liver.

5.1 Pregnant women drink alcohol.
5.2 They put unborn children at serious risk.

6.1 Millions of adults drink responsibly.
6.2 Serious problems result from overuse.
6.3 The problems are related to alcohol.

7.1 Alcohol causes 100,000 deaths annually.
7.2 Deaths result from various diseases.
7.3 They include cirrhosis of the liver.
7.4 Deaths result from traffic accidents.

8.1 Fatalities declined during the 1980s.
8.2 They were caused by drunk drivers.
8.3 This was thanks to public pressure.
8.4 Alcohol still contributes to 50,000 deaths.
8.5 Alcohol still contributes to 500,000 injuries.
8.6 These occur each year on our highways.

Writing Tip   In clusters 3 and 5, try using *who* as a connector. Do not use commas with these clauses.

Invitation   Develop a character sketch or dramatic incident to introduce "Alcohol Facts" and "More Alcohol Facts."

⊃ *More Alcohol Facts*

Directions "Alcohol Facts" precedes this exercise. Combine sentences to create the *third* of four paragraphs. Then work on the Invitation below for the *fourth* paragraph.

1.1 The body metabolizes alcohol slowly.
1.2 Nothing can be done to speed the process.

2.1 Running does not sober you up.
2.2 Eating a meal does not sober you up.
2.3 Drinking coffee does not sober you up.
2.4 Taking a shower does not sober you up.
2.5 This is contrary to popular opinion.

3.1 Alcohol has been carefully studied.
3.2 Basic physiological facts are well known.

4.1 The drug affects the nervous system.
4.2 It impairs judgment.
4.3 It impairs memory.
4.4 It impairs sensory perception.

5.1 It also depresses brain functions.
5.2 The functions integrate behavior.
5.3 It causes jumbled thoughts.
5.4 It causes reduced concentration.

6.1 Alcohol promotes sleepiness.
6.2 It also disrupts sleep patterns.
6.3 It also disrupts dream patterns.

7.1 Alcohol acts as a diuretic.
7.2 It stimulates the kidneys to pass water.
7.3 Heavy drinkers often experience dehydration.

8.1 The "hangover" has only one real cure.
8.2 It consists of dry mouth.
8.3 It consists of sour stomach.
8.4 It consists of headache.
8.5 It consists of fatigue.
8.6 The cure is the passage of time.

Writing Tip In cluster 2, change the verb *does* to *do* if you create a compound subject. In clusters 1 and 7, try *because* as a connector.

Invitation Write a concluding paragraph for "Alcohol Facts" and "More Alcohol Facts." Share your text with a writing partner, and use his or her feedback to revise.

⊃ *Genetic Defects*

Directions Combine sentences to create the *first* of four paragraphs. Then work on the Invitation below for the *second* paragraph. "Genetic Counseling" follows this exercise.

1.1 Scientific evidence has accumulated.
1.2 It supports a grim hypothesis.
1.3 The human species is becoming weaker.
1.4 The weakening is genetic.

2.1 Many scientists now believe something.
2.2 Genetic deterioration is inevitable.
2.3 Defective babies now survive.
2.4 The babies once would have perished.

3.1 Defects have an effect.
3.2 The defects are hereditary.
3.3 The effect is cumulative.
3.4 The effect "snowballs."
3.5 This is according to experts.

4.1 The population grows.
4.2 Defects increase.
4.3 The increase is geometric.

5.1 Increases occur in three generations.
5.2 The increases are substantial.
5.3 The increases are in defective babies.

6.1 These defects are passed on.
6.2 They become multiplied again and again.

7.1 Modern medicine is a triumph.
7.2 It was achieved by human intelligence.
7.3 That triumph may have created problems.
7.4 The problems are horrendous.
7.5 The problems are for the future.

8.1 Medicine has upset the natural balance.
8.2 Technology has upset the natural balance.
8.3 Our survival capacity may be diminished.

Writing Tip   In cluster 1, try a colon or dash for emphasis. In cluster 8, note that a compound subject requires a changed verb.

Invitation   Provide a graphic example of a serious genetic defect (for example, muscular dystrophy) that will serve as a link to the "Genetic Counseling" exercise that follows.

⊃ *Genetic Counseling*

Directions "Genetic Defects" precedes this exercise. Combine sentences to create the *third* of four paragraphs. Then work on the Invitation below for the *fourth* paragraph.

1.1 Prospective parents can get advice.
1.2 They have concerns about birth defects.
1.3 The advice is from genetic counseling centers.
1.4 Centers are located throughout North America.

2.1 These people may come from families.
2.2 The families have a history of defects.
2.3 They may already have produced a child.
2.4 The child has an inherited problem.

3.1 Such centers provide information.
3.2 Information enables parents to make decisions.
3.3 The decisions are intelligent.
3.4 The decisions are socially responsible.

4.1 Genetic counseling has been successful.
4.2 The counseling is voluntary.
4.3 Some people now argue for genetic screening.
4.4 The screening would be mandatory.

5.1 Such a system would grant "birth permits."
5.2 The permits would be to certain parents.
5.3 The parents are free of genetic defects.
5.4 It would withhold permits from others.
5.5 The others carry diseases.
5.6 The diseases are hereditary.

6.1 Proponents acknowledge something.
6.2 Mandatory screening would be expensive.
6.3 It would curtail personal fredoms.
6.4 We take personal freedoms for granted.

7.1 But they contend something.
7.2 The benefits outweigh the costs.
7.3 The benefits are reduced human suffering.
7.4 The benefits are a stronger gene pool.

Writing Tip   Delete *something* in sentences 6.1 and 7.1, and use *that* as a connector. In cluster 7, try a pair of dashes for emphasis.

Invitation   Write a concluding paragraph for "Genetic Defects" and "Genetic Counseling" that sums up the problem. Share your text with a writing partner, and use his or her feedback to revise.

⊃ *Marijuana Facts*

Directions   Combine sentences to create the *second* of four paragraphs. Then work on the Invitation below for the *first* paragraph. "More Marijuana Facts" follows this exercise.

1.1 Many teenagers believe something.
1.2 Marijuana is relatively safe.
1.3 The facts suggest otherwise.

2.1 Use of the drug affects memory.
2.2 It affects one's sense of time.
2.3 It affects the ability to think.
2.4 It affects the ability to feel.

3.1 It also reduces coordination.
3.2 It also reduces concentration.
3.3 These are essential for driving.
3.4 These are essential for other tasks.

4.1 The drug weakens the motivation center.
4.2 The motivation center is in the brain.
4.3 The drug can cause permanent damage.

5.1 Typical results include listlessness.
5.2 They include learning difficulties.
5.3 They include an inability to cope.

6.1 It can also produce acute panic.
6.2 It can produce paranoia.
6.3 It can produce flashbacks.
6.4 It can produce hallucinations.

7.1 Marijuana is more harmful than tobacco.
7.2 Its smoke contains more carbon monoxide.
7.3 Its smoke contains more chemicals.
7.4 The chemicals are cancer-causing.

8.1 Inhaling the smoke can lead to emphysema.
8.2 Inhaling the smoke can lead to bronchitis.
8.3 The bronchitis is chronic.
8.4 These shorten one's life span.

Writing Tip In cluster 1, delete *something* and use *that* as a connector. In clusters 2, 5, and 6, punctuate three or more items in a series.

Invitation Create a brief character sketch or dramatic incident to introduce "Marijuana Facts" and "More Marijuana Facts."

⊃ *More Marijuana Facts*

Directions "Marijuana Facts" precedes this exercise. Combine sentences to create the *third* of four paragraphs. Then work on the Invitation below for the *fourth* paragraph.

1.1 "Potheads" develop a tolerance.
1.2 "Potheads" use the drug regularly.
1.3 The tolerance is for marijuana.

2.1 They need increasing amounts to get high.
2.2 They develop a dependence on the drug.
2.3 The dependence is psychological.

3.1 Not all potheads progress to other drugs.
3.2 Over half "graduate" to a drug-free life.
3.3 Sixty percent is the exact number.

4.1 Withdrawal symptoms appear to be mild.
4.2 The withdrawal is from marijuana.
4.3 Many people conclude something.
4.4 The conclusion is erroneous.
4.5 The drug is not addictive.

5.1 The facts suggest something.
5.2 Marijuana is stored in body tissues.
5.3 Storage is for several months.
5.4 It continues to affect metabolism.

6.1 Marijuana produces the chemcal THC.
6.2 Researchers have studied THC extensively.
6.3 They have conducted controlled experiments.

7.1 Health scientists now know something.
7.2 THC lingers in body cells for 30 days.
7.3 This is after a *single* marijuana cigarette.
7.4 Chemical traces can still be detected.
7.5 The detection is 145 days later.

8.1 This is an important fact to know.
8.2 One is employed by a company.
8.3 The company screens for drug use.

Writing Tip   In clusters 5 and 7, delete *something* in sentences 5.1 and 7.1. Use *that* connectors to make parallel clauses.

Invitation Write a concluding paragraph for "Marijuana Facts" and "More Marijuana Facts." Share your text with a writing partner, and use his or her feedback to revise.

⊃ *Japanese Schools*

Directions Combine sentences to create the *first* of four paragraphs. Then work on the Invitation below for the *second* paragraph. "Education Commitment" follows this exercise.

1.1 Japanese schools reflect a society.
1.2 The society stresses literacy.
1.3 The society values excellence.
1.4 The excellence is in education.

2.1 High school attendance is not compulsory.
2.2 Ninety-eight percent choose to attend.
2.3 Ninety-nine percent achieve literacy.

3.1 Japan's graduation rate is 90 percent.
3.2 This compares with a 75 percent rate in the United States.

4.1 Teenagers graduate from Japanese high schools.
4.2 Many know as much as average college graduates.
4.3 The college graduates are in the United States.

5.1 Teenagers graduate from American high schools.
5.2 One in ten is functionally illiterate.
5.3 One in ten is ill-equipped for survival.

6.1 International tests indicate something.
6.2 Japanese students outperform all others.
6.3 This is particularly in math.
6.4 This is particularly in science.
6.5 These hold the keys to future technologies.

7.1 Japan has half the population of the United States.
7.2 It produces 9 percent more engineers each year.
7.3 This is a worrisome fact to Americans.
7.4 The Americans track our competitiveness.

8.1 The Japanese believe something.
8.2 Education is a top national priority.
8.3 Effort is a major factor in learning.
8.4 Cooperation is a major factor in learning.
8.5 Self-discipline is a major factor in learning.

Writing Tip In cluster 8, delete the word *something* in sentence 8.1. Use *that* to make two parallel clauses.

Invitation Create a paragraph that explores the possible threat to U.S. security as introduced by the "Japanese Schools" exercise. Then go on to the "Education Commitment" exercise.

⊃ *Education Commitment*

Directions "Japanese Schools" precedes this exercise. Combine sentences to create the *third* of four paragraphs. Then work on the Invitation below for the *fourth* paragraph.

1.1 Americans pay lip service to education
1.2 The Japanese act on their beliefs.
1.3 They do this in several ways.

2.1 Japanese schools run 240 days a year.
2.2 This is 60 days more than the American school year.

3.1 Mothers teach children to be gentle.
3.2 They teach children to be alert.
3.3 They teach children to be open-minded.
3.4 They also stress the value of cooperation.

4.1 Japanese parents buy books each month.
4.2 The books are for preschoolers.
4.3 They use many games and activities.
4.4 These are to teach literacy skills.

5.1 Teachers receive high salaries.
5.2 They are always accorded status.
5.3 They are always accorded respect.
5.4 Their work is seen as vital.

6.1 Japanese classes are large.
6.2 The classes average about 40 students.
6.3 Teachers take great pride in their work.
6.4 They have few discipline problems.

7.1 Teachers talk frequently with parents.
7.2 The parents encourage their children to study.
7.3 The parents pay for special classes.
7.4 The classes occur after school.

8.1 And Japanese students do their part.
8.2 They watch relatively little TV.
8.3 They study hard for examinations.
8.4 The examinations determine future careers.

Writing Tip In clusters 1 and 6, try several connectors—*but, yet, while, although, however*—before settling on one.

Invitation Write a concluding paragraph for "Japanese Schools" and "Education Commitment." Share your text with a writing partner, and use his or her feedback to revise.

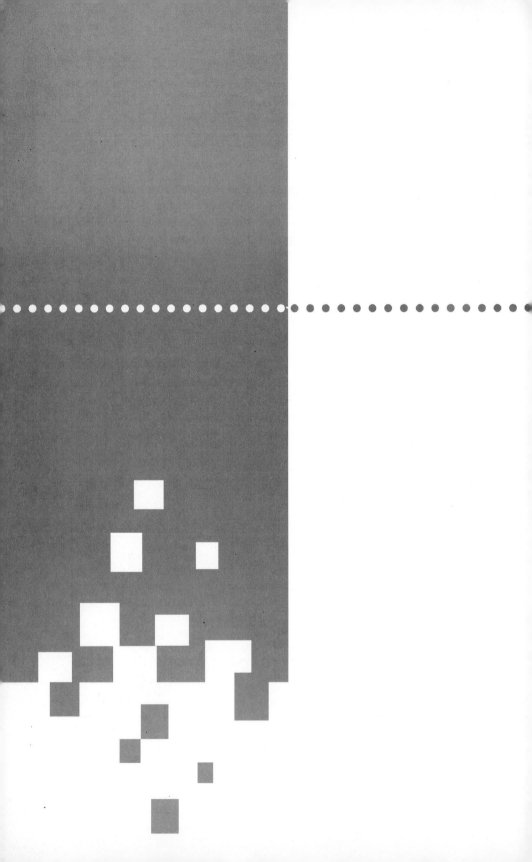

Unclustered

Combining

"How can I know what I think 'til I see what I say?" The question posed by novelist E. M. Forster is a good one when you stop to think about it. Sometimes we don't know what we think until our words are arrayed before us, awkward and tentative and incomplete, and we pause to look them over. It is this act that helps thinking take increasingly clear shape.

The more that you regard writing as a *thinking* process—a way of discovering meaning—the more interesting it becomes. One part of discovery is the first draft, of course. But even more exciting to many writers is the process of tinkering with meanings on the page (or word processor screen). Sometimes you can sharpen a point by adding details; sometimes you can make sentences easier to read by rearranging them; and sometimes you can delete words, phrases, or irrelevant sentences to achieve a tight, clear focus.

In Unit 4 we explore the process of tinkering with paragraphs. You'll have a change to add details, rearrange sentences, and take out information that seems irrelevant to the topic at hand. But this section of combining differs from exercises in other units. Here it's your task to decide "what goes with what." You can make sentences as long or as short as you choose and arrange them in whatever ways seem interesting.

A PROCESS OF TINKERING

Let's look at an unclustered SC exercise to demonstrate how the process of "tinkering" works. Take a few moments to scan this brief descriptive passage and decide "what goes with what."

1. The Frisbee is flicked sideways with a motion.
2. The motion is quick and snakelike.
3. It spins clockwise.
4. It is saucerlike.
5. It rides a puddle of air.
6. It slices through sunlight.
7. It slices through shadows.
8. It glides across a grassy clearing.
9. Then a breeze catches the disk.
10. The breeze makes it climb and dip.
11. It follows the surface currents.
12. It whirls soundlessly.
13. It drops lower and lower.
14. It settles onto my index finger.
15. My finger is outstretched.

Perhaps you've spotted some "natural breaks" in the sequence above. Our aim in working with this exercise is to produce *good* sentences, ones that capture the action.

Let's now take a careful look at the differences among three versions that have been prepared for you. Which one do you, as a reader, think best captures the action being described?

VERSION X. (1) The spinning, saucerlike Frisbee rides a puddle of air after being flicked sideways with a quick and snakelike motion. (2) Slicing through sunlight and shadows, it glides across a grassy clearing. (3) Then a breeze catches the disk and makes it climb and dip, following the surface currents. (4) As it whirls soundlessly, dropping lower and lower, it finally settles on my outstretched index finger.

VERSION Y. (1) Flicked sideways with a quick, snakelike motion, the Frisbee spins clockwise, its saucerlike shape riding a puddle of air. (2) It slices through sunlight and shadows, gliding across a grassy clearing, and catches a breeze. (3) Then it climbs and dips to follow the surface currents, whirling lower and lower toward my outstretched index finger, where it settles soundlessly.

VERSION Z. (1) Like a sentinel, my outstretched index finger awaits the Frisbee. (2) It glides saucerlike through sunlight and shadows, riding a puddle of air. (3) As it slices across a grassy clearing, a breeze catches the disk, making it climb and dip. (4) It follows the surface currents, the invisible waves and barbecue smells of a Sunday afternoon. (5) Whirling lower and lower, it finally settles soundlessly, right on target. (6) Then I flick it back, quick and snakelike.

As you know by now, each of these versions has its own unique virtues. While you may prefer Version Z because it adds details that enrich the description, you probably see that both Version X and Version Y have their own interesting features. What matters is the process of creating and comparing paragraphs like these.

A PERSONAL WRITING STYLE

The process described above—deciding "what goes with what," then tinkering with paragraph organization as well as sentence construction—is one that can teach you more about your own style of writing. By comparing your paragraphs with those of other students, you will begin to see patterns in your prose.

In doing the exercises in Unit 4, you'll find it helpful to read through an entire list of sentences before combining any of them. With the sequence in mind, look for logical "breaks" or "clusters" of meaning. Check these points lightly with a pencil. Put a question mark in areas where you're uncertain.

As you compare your paragraphs with those written by others, try to see where other writers have clustered, rearranged, or deleted sentences. If you find paragraphs that you particularly like, ask questions of your workshop partners. Get them to verbalize their thinking/writing process so you can learn from what they do.

The point of unclustered combining, remember, is not to make long sentences but rather to make *good* ones. Don't try to put all kernel sentences into one gigantic "supersentence." Instead, work for clarity, variety, and creativity in your paragraphs. After completing some work that represents you well, team up with others to make comparisons. Look for patterns in your writing style.

⊃ *Chain Saw*

Personification gives human (or animal) attributes to things or ideas. Watch for personification as you combine.

1. The chain saw snarls and bucks.
2. It bites through white fir.
3. It spits out chunks of wood.
4. High above are swaying branches.
5. They seem to tremble back and forth.
6. The saw bites deeper.
7. It makes its final cut.
8. The fir tree now groans.
9. The fir tree now begins to teeter.
10. The saw rips still deeper.
11. It tears at the fir's heartwood.
12. The tree sways again.
13. It hesitates breathlessly.
14. A shudder passes down its length.
15. The saw shuts down with a gasp.
16. The fir's groan becomes a cracking.

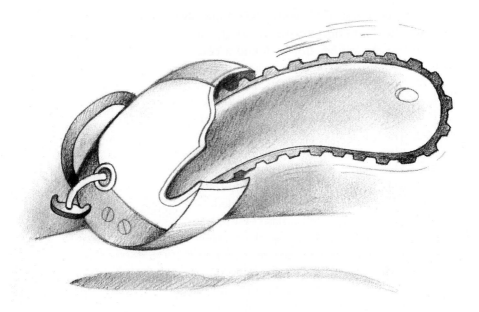

17. The cracking is long and splintered.
18. Its inner core gives way to gravity.
19. Its lean is imperceptible at first.
20. Gravity's pull is inexorable.

Invitation Finish this description of the falling fir tree, continuing the use of personification.

⊃ *Desperate Chef*

When George's wife is away, he must fend for himself. Once again, he meets the challenge with characteristic manly grace.

1. George wandered into the kitchen.
2. He took a recipe book from the shelf.

3. He thumbed its worn pages aimlessly.
4. In the refrigerator he found dry carrots.
5. In the refrigerator he found a potato.
6. In the refrigerator he found limp celery.
7. In the refrigerator he found yellow onions.
8. In the refrigerator he found flank steak.
9. The steak was just on the edge of spoiling.
10. He promptly cut up all of this.
11. He heated an iron kettle on the stove.
12. He seared the red cubes of beef.
13. He added two handfuls of onions.
14. The onions steamed and sizzled.
15. George then felt a flash of inspiration.
16. George uncorked a bottle of cheap red wine.
17. He splashed its dregs into the kettle.
18. The kitchen now reeked of charred meat.
19. George smiled in a satisfied way.
20. George added the stew's final ingredients.

Invitation   Describe how George prepares a dessert to accompany this elegant supper; or describe the kitchen's aftermath.

⊃ Hawaiian Hula

The chanter recites to the rhythmic beating of a drum, and dancers swirl and sway as one, interpreting the past. Welcome to the hula.

1. Hawaii is famous for the hula.
2. The hula is an elegant dance.
3. It expresses the culture of the islands.
4. It expresses the history of the islands.
5. It expresses the stories of the islands.
6. Missionaries suppressed this native dance.
7. This was during the nineteenth century.
8. They did not understand its complexity.
9. They did not understand its significance.

10. It was saved from extinction by Kalākaua.
11. Kalākaua was a Hawaiian monarch.
12. He called it "the language of the heart."
13. Today's Hawaiians perform two types of hula.
14. Each has its unique style.
15. The ancient style is called hula *kahiko*.
16. It is accompanied only by chanting.
17. It is accompanied only by drumming.
18. The modern style is called hula *auana*.
19. It is more fluid and sensuous.
20. It is accompanied by musical instruments.

Invitation Speculate on the motives of missionaries for suppressing the expression of native Hawaiians; then comment on the morality of such actions from today's perspective.

⊃ Opposite Personalities

Do you have friends or family members who almost always see things in a positive (or negative) light? How do *you* see things?

1. The world has two kinds of people.
2. One kind is the optimist.
3. The other kind is the pessimist.
4. An optimist is a person.
5. The person sees a water glass.
6. The water glass is partially filled.
7. The person declares it "half full."
8. A pessimist sees the same glass.
9. The pessimist declares it "half empty."
10. Such statements describe differences in perception.
11. Such statements describe differences in personality.
12. The differences are not in physical reality.
13. Optimism is a way of seeing the world.
14. Optimism is a way of processing the world.
15. So is pessimism.

16. Pessimism is the alternative view.
17. Both have influences on human behavior.
18. The influences are profound.
19. A brief illustration should clarify this point.
20. The illustration is personal.

Invitation Develop a follow-up illustration from your own experience to clarify the ideas being introduced in this paragraph. Show how *attitude* can shape behavior.

⊃ Morning Shower

One way to hook reader interest is to use strategic surprise. Here is a quiet, relaxed scene—a backdrop for a personal decision.

1. She was in the shower.
2. A warm torrent burbled over her head.

3. It foamed sheets of water down her body.
4. She relaxed under the noise.
5. She was unable to think about anything.
6. Her consciousness was focused on the spray.
7. The spray was prickly.
8. The spray needled her back.
9. She hummed to herself.
10. She turned slowly under the showerhead.
11. The showerhead gushed.
12. It was as if she were basting on a barbecue.
13. The air tasted wet and clean.
14. She closed her eyes.
15. The world seemed simple.
16. The simplicity was perfect.
17. It was without anger.
18. It was without accusations.
19. It was without thoughtless remarks.
20. There was nothing but sensation.
21. The sensation was pure.
22. She stood that way for a long time.
23. She listened to the sound of water.
24. The water gurgled down the drain.
25. She knew what she had to do.

Invitation Extend this narrative by imagining what the young woman's decision is. You may wish to use your own experience as you develop this story.

⊃ *Orchard Memory*

The sense of smell can trigger deep memories. Try to remember the smells of fresh-baked bread, chalk trays in school, juicy apples.

1. The orchard stood behind a white frame house.
2. The house belonged to my grandparents.
3. My grandfather had planted it.
4. He had cared for it most of his life.
5. This was in spite of Grandma's protests.

6. Its trees were gnarled and bent.
7. Its trees were not very productive.
8. They left me with great memories.
9. I could explore a new tree each day.
10. I could listen to the bees work.
11. This was my favorite place in late summer.
12. This was my favorite place in early fall.
13. The days were long and sleepy.
14. I could wander by myself.
15. I could play with my friends.
16. Apples hung heavy from the boughs.
17. They were ready for picking.
18. I remember the air as sweet.
19. I remember the air as heavy.
20. It was full of green shadows.
21. It smell of ripe fruit.
22. I wiped the apple juice.
23. The juice ran down my chin.
24. I could see leaves beginning to curl.
25. I could see leaves beginning to turn golden.

Invitation Think of a favorite place from your childhood. Be there again, recalling smells if possible. Write about this place from a first-person ("I") point of view.

⊃ *Winning Attitude*

Coaches talk about a winning attitude. Is there such a thing? Can you feel it sometimes in other people? What is a winning attitude?

1. Mona sees herself as a winner.
2. Mona sees herself not as a loser.
3. Her self-image is strong and upbeat.
4. Her self-image is decidedly optimistic.
5. She knows her strengths.
6. She acknowledges her weaknesses.
7. She sets goals for herself.
8. The goals are realistic and achievable.
9. Her toughness comes from an attitude.
10. Her attitude is resilient.
11. It tells her to bounce back.
12. Things don't go her way.
13. She learns from her difficulties.
14. She doesn't take them personally.
15. She doesn't let them demoralize her.
16. She sees mistakes as learning opportunities.
17. She doesn't regard them as traumatic events.
18. Mona has average talents.
19. Mona has ordinary levels of skill.
20. Mona has unusual personal poise.
21. This is for one simple reason.
22. She knows who she is.
23. She likes who she is.
24. She long ago realized something.
25. Winning is a state of mind.
26. It is a willingness to persevere.
27. It is a reluctance to give up.
28. This attitude makes her a team player.

29. The attitude is aggressively positive.
30. The player pulls her weight at the office.
31. The player gives to her community.
32. Mona will ultimately succeed.
33. She has the right attitude toward life.
34. "Be a winner."
35. "Don't be a whiner."

Invitation In a follow-up paragraph, contrast Mona with a person who is a "loser" in his or her approach to life. Try to develop your character sketch with specific, vivid examples.

⊃ *Ginseng Special*

Visiting a health food store, you're sure to see advertisements for *ginseng*. But what is it? And is it for you?

1. Ginseng has been used for over 5000 years.
2. *Ginseng* means "manroot" in Chinese.
3. Its use has been mainly in the Orient.
4. The root has been called "the elixir of life."
5. It supposedly possesses medicinal powers.
6. The powers are extraordinary.
7. The powers improve one's health.
8. Ginseng is like Geritol in many Asian households.
9. Ginseng is like aspirin in many Asian households.
10. Ginseng is used to remedy "tired blood."
11. Ginseng is used to treat pain.
12. Ginseng is used to treat flagging virility.
13. The root is widely available today.
14. It is often soaking in water or rice wine.
15. This has not always been the case.
16. Ginseng was once regarded as royal property.
17. Ginseng was exchanged between royal families.
18. Ginseng was a symbol of respect.
19. Commoners were severely punished.

20. The commoners possessed ginseng.
21. Today it is available in tea.
22. It is available in soft drinks.
23. It is available in dried form.
24. It can also be eaten raw.
25. It can be cooked in other foods.
26. It can be boiled to make an extract.
27. Many Westerners remain skeptical of ginseng.
28. They dismiss its reported claims.
29. Some scientists continue to study its properties.
30. The scientists are Russian.
31. The properties are health-related.

Invitation   Visit a health food store to learn more about the cost of ginseng—brace yourself—and its properties. Put what you learn into a follow-up paragraph.

ꓛ *Tying the Knot*

A marriage marks a turning point, "for better or for worse," in the life story of many people. Make a prediction about this one.

1. The groom waits in the church vestibule.
2. His waiting is anxious.
3. The groom tries to smile.
4. Sweat stands out on his forehead.
5. He blinks.
6. He fidgets with his black bow tie.
7. The cue comes from the organist.
8. The best man opens the door.
9. The two take their places at the altar.
10. The altar is opposite the oak pulpit.
11. Eyes turn toward the groom.
12. The eyes are silent.
13. He glances toward the church entrance.
14. People are clustered there.
15. The bride appears in a silk gown.
16. The silk is milk-white.
17. The bridesmaids lead the procession.
18. They rustle down the center aisle.
19. They wear dresses of yellow pastels.
20. They carry bouquets of fresh daisies.
21. The daisies look like sunny faces.
22. Familiar music swells through the church.
23. The music is "Here Comes the Bride."
24. Behind her veil the bride bites her lip.
25. The bride manages a brave smile.
26. Her father looks on.
27. Her father is a stern man.
28. The man is shovel-faced.
29. She approaches the altar.
30. Her future husband awaits.

Invitation You can extend this narrative with additional description or use it to introduce your views about marriage and divorce in today's world.

⊃ *Parable 3*

Writers have long used fables and parables to make important points in subtle and memorable ways. What is the point here?

1. A fruit seller once lived in Hangchow.
2. The seller knew how to keep oranges.
3. The oranges kept for a whole year.
4. They did not wither or spoil.
5. The fruit always looked fresh.
6. The fruit always looked firm.
7. It was actually dry inside.
8. Its dryness was like an old cocoon.
9. Something happened one day.
10. A customer criticized the seller.
11. The customer was irate.
12. The criticism was loud.
13. "You have created an illusion."
14. "The illusion is outrageous."
15. "The illusion deceives the public."
16. "Your only purpose is to cheat fools."
17. "The fools have worked hard for their money."

18. The seller replied in this way.
19. The seller was hunched and wrinkled.
20. "Our officials sit in lofty halls."
21. "They ride magnificent horses."
22. "They get drunk on fine wine."
23. "They stuff themselves with succulent food."
24. "Our officials know no shame."
25. "They eat the bread of state."
26. "They instead put on awe-inspiring looks."
27. "The looks are an illusory display of greatness."
28. "The looks are an illusory display of worth."
29. Then the seller laughed.
30. "You pay no heed to things of importance."
31. "You are concerned about matters."
32. "The matters are trivial."

Invitation   Try to generalize (or draw a moral) from this simple parable. What do you take as its "point"?

⊃ Karate Explained

How is it that some people can break boards and bricks with their hands? Read on and combine.

1. Karate is an ancient Asian art.
2. It means "empty hand."
3. It involves using body parts.
4. The use is to break hard objects.
5. Okinawa was occupied by Japanese samurai.
6. This was during the seventeenth century.
7. Citizens turned their hands into weapons.
8. Citizens turned their feet into weapons.
9. The weapons could smash bamboo armor.
10. A karate "chop" involves a thrust.
11. The thrust is short and sharp.
12. The hand remains as rigid as possible.
13. Its rigidity is at the moment of impact.
14. The same principle holds for the foot.

15. The foot delivers more force.
16. It has greater mass.
17. A karate expert uses his entire body.
18. This is when delivering a blow.
19. This chop must be extremely short.
20. This chop must be extremely swift.
21. This is to accomplish its task.
22. This is to prevent bodily injury.
23. Contact with a brick lasts for only a flash.
24. It is less than ten one-thousandths of a second.
25. The hand recoils at nearly 200 miles per hour.
26. A human hand can withstand a ton of force.
27. The hand has highly elastic bones.
28. It must be rigid and quick to do so.

Invitation Can you apply the underlying principles of karate to other areas of your physical, mental, or spiritual life?

⊃ World Population

Twenty million people now live in Mexico City. And the situation will get much worse before it gets better. Why is this?

1. The world's population continues to grow.
2. The rate of growth is alarming.
3. This is particularly in Third World countries.
4. The level of poverty is staggering.
5. Population passed 1 billion in 1800.
6. It passed 2 billion in 1920.
7. It passed 3 billion in 1960.
8. World population today numbers 5 billion.
9. It will increase to 8 billion by 2025.
10. Present rates suggest a doubling of population.
11. The doubling is within 35 years.
12. About 95 percent of this will be in the Third World.
13. Bangladesh is smaller than Wisconsin.
14. Bangladesh now supports 115 million people.
15. Bangladesh will face 250 million people by 2025.

16. Mexico faces similar population pressures.
17. Mexico now has about 85 million people.
18. It will have 150 million hungry mouths by 2025.
19. Equally bleak is the situation in India.
20. India presently has 880 million people.
21. It will eventually surpass China.
22. China now has 1.17 billion people.
23. China now has a slower growth rate.
24. Populations are also exploding in Africa.
25. Populations are also exploding in Latin America.
26. These areas have seen overgrazing.
27. These areas have seen soil erosion.
28. These areas have seen forest destruction.
29. Such damage has long-term consequences.
30. The damage is to the environment.
31. It increases the possibility of famines.
32. The famines would be catastrophic.

33. The famines would be similar to those in Somalia.
34. Overcrowding also leads to flows of refugees.
35. The flows are ceaseless.
36. The flows are into industrialized countries.
37. The industrialized countries cannot handle them.
38. World population is like a time bomb.
39. The time bomb is ticking.
40. Natural resources are dwindling.
41. Population pressures are rapidly increasing.

Invitation   Should the United States take an active role in helping Third World nations to control world population growth? What specific dangers do you see in unrestrained growth in world population?

⊃ First Light

It's the hour before dawn when night reaches its darkest point—like a black velvet backdrop for an unfolding array of first light.

1. The night had been black.
2. It had been brittle-cold.
3. It had been pierced by slivers of light.
4. The light was from the city.
5. Trains rumbled in the switchyard.
6. They moved freight down steel rails.
7. The rails glittered.
8. A siren wailed in the distance.
9. Its sound rose and fell.
10. Its sound trailed off into silence.
11. The silence was empty.
12. Taxicabs rolled down streets.
13. The streets were bare and deserted.
14. The desertion seemed ominous.
15. Their headlights fanned the buildings.
16. Garbage trucks made their rounds.
17. The rounds were preappointed.
18. The rounds were nightly.
19. They lumbered past alleys.

20. The homeless huddled in packing crates.
21. The packing crates were cardboard.
22. The homeless tried to keep warm.
23. Then the blackness began to soften.
24. The blackness was in the east.
25. It became a deep charcoal gray.
26. The gray was the color of soot.
27. The sky lightened further.
28. It revealed the outline of buildings.
29. They were black against the horizon.
30. Gray then warmed to a soft grayish rose.
31. It was like the stain of old wine.
32. Dawn backlighted a layer of clouds.
33. Dawn worked its way across the horizon.
34. The work was inexorable.
35. The light was alabaster and white.
36. The light was pink and pale yellow.
37. It was like the inside of an oyster shell.
38. "This is incredible," the director whispered.
39. Her smile stretched ear to ear.
40. The cameraman narrowed his eyes.
41. The cameraman touched his forehead.
42. "Uh, I think I forgot to load the camera."

Invitation Do you know about great expectations and missed opportunities? Focus on this idea as you parallel "First Light."

ꜛ *Video Dating*

Can you see yourself shopping for companionship through a catalog? Outrageous? Maybe in the Age of AIDS the idea has more merit.

1. Video dating is an approach to romance.
2. The approach is scientific.
3. It helps some people meet new friends.
4. This is for a membership fee.
5. Clients fill out questionnaires.
6. The questionnaires are about themselves.

7. The questionnaires are called Member Profiles.
8. Clients are then interviewed on videotape.
9. Member Profiles are filed in a notebook.
10. The notebook is alphabetized.
11. One uses the notebook as a card catalog.
12. The catalog is for the videotape library.
13. One first reads biographical information.
14. One then views various videotapes.
15. The videotapes are for prospective dates.
16. One makes a tentative selection.
17. The dating service sends the client a card.
18. The client then comes to the dating service.
19. The client examines the chooser's Member Profile.
20. The client views the chooser's videotape.
21. The client decides whether to accept a date.
22. The dating service releases phone numbers.
23. The release is on one condition.
24. Both parties want to meet.
25. No date can be arranged without this agreement.
26. The dating service protects clients' identities.
27. It assigns each person an ID number.
28. Advocates of the service contend this.
29. Video dating provides one-stop shopping.
30. The shopping is for consumers.
31. The consumers are value-oriented.
32. It offers a rational alternative.
33. The alternative is to barhopping.
34. The alternative is to church socials.
35. It is here to stay.

Invitation   Video dating is alive and well in many big cities. In follow-up writing, prepare a Member Profile for yourself. Or, if you'd prefer, discuss what video dating reveals about our society.

⊃ *Apartment 7*

How can you use writing to take readers on a "guided tour" of a physical location? It helps to focus on specific details.

1. Apartment 7 had been the height of fashion.
2. The fashion was 25 years ago.
3. Now it just looked faded and tired.
4. Now it just looked a little cluttered.
5. There was a faded Oriental carpet.
6. It covered oak squares in the living room.
7. There were paperback books on pine shelves.
8. The pine shelves had brick spacers.
9. There was a curtain of colored beads.
10. There was a Tiffany-style lamp.
11. The lamp was made from a kit.
12. The walls were decorated with posters.
13. The walls were bone-white.
14. The posters showed faraway destinations.
15. The posters showed gray beaches.
16. The beaches were shrouded by fog.

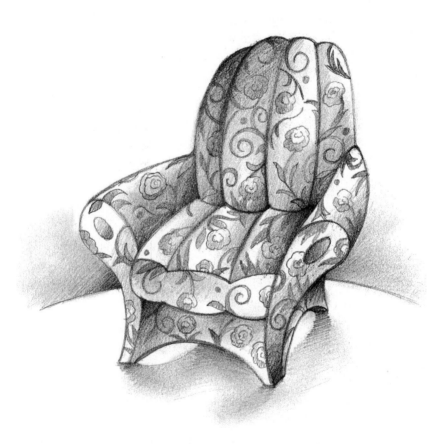

17. A smell of incense filled the room.
18. It was faint and exotic.
19. In the corner stood a wooden cabinet.
20. It held an ancient FM tuner.
21. It held a tape deck with an open lid.
22. It held uneven stacks of cassette tapes.
23. The furniture was odds and ends.
24. It had no unifying theme.
25. There was an overstuffed chair.
26. It had a floral covering.
27. There was a sofa bed.
28. It had seen better days.
29. There was a pair of bentwood chairs.
30. There was a small kitchen table.
31. It doubled as a desk.
32. Apartment 7 was not like my place.
33. My place was across town.
34. I would get used to its quirkiness.
35. Its quirkiness was a throwback to the 1970s.

Invitation Using "Apartment 7" as model, describe the place where you live. Imagine a camera scanning the room. To organize this writing, move systematically, positioning objects for the reader.

⊃ Homeless

Have you ever wondered about the life stories of homeless people you see in any American city? How did they get there? And why?

1. The public library closes its doors.
2. A homeless man heads out into a cold night.
3. Neon lights flicker against the sky.
4. The traffic flows by in a stream.
5. The stream is ceaseless.
6. His tiredness is a numb ache.
7. It stretches down his back.
8. It reaches all the way to his feet.
9. Above the storefronts are buildings.

10. The storefronts are barricaded.
11. The buildings are faceless.
12. The buildings house offices.
13. The offices are like the one he once knew.
14. His life now feels like a bad dream.
15. The dream has no awakening.
16. It has no room for family or friends.
17. His focus is survival.
18. His focus is one meal at a time.
19. His focus is a safe place out of the wind.
20. He can close his eyes there.
21. Now he pulls a wool cap over his ears.
22. He turns up his jacket collar.
23. He jams gloved fists deep into his pockets.
24. He shuffles toward the Gospel Mission.
25. It is a place of refuge.
26. The refuge is temporary.
27. Hunger is his constant companion.
28. Loneliness is his constant companion.
29. He has never been a good panhandler.
30. Tonight he feels more desperate than usual.
31. He hangs out near a fast-food restaurant.

32. He coaxes a quarter here and there.
33. This is until the police run him off.
34. Then he coughs into his clenched fists.
35. He slips the coins into his boot.
36. He stumbles off toward the Mission.

Invitation Write about this man's story as you imagine it (or as you know it from the stories of others). Does such a story make you worry about your own future—or the future of those you love?

⊃ *Black Holes*

Some people speculate that black holes are points of entry to other universes—or to the past or future in our own universe. Read on.

1. Black holes are dying stars.
2. The stars have collapsed inward.
3. They have created pits in space.
4. The pits are bottomless.
5. Nothing can escape black holes.
6. Not even light can escape black holes.
7. Light travels at 186,000 miles per second.
8. They are called "the last laugh of the cosmos."
9. The black hole has a gravitational pull.
10. The gravitational pull is incredible.
11. It sucks up all matter within reach.
12. It sucks up all energy within reach.
13. It is like a cosmic vacuum cleaner.
14. Scientists infer that black holes exist.
15. Light cannot escape them.
16. X-ray measurements provide observational data.
17. Current theories suggest something.
18. Matter emits x-rays.
19. Matter swirls around a black hole.
20. Matter is heated to billions of degrees.
21. Such x-ray emissions were first detected in 1967.
22. Detection was in the constellation Cygnus.
23. Similar findings have since occurred elsewhere.

24. Scientists now believe something.
25. Deep inside each black hole is "singularity."
26. "Singularity" is a region of extreme density.
27. The laws of physics break down there.
28. A teaspoon of matter weighs billions of tons.
29. Our galaxy's hole may be three times our sun's mass.
30. It may be less than one-fiftieth its size.

Invitation Congratulations! NASA has invited you to participate in a mission "that will explore the perimeter of a newly discovered black hole." Accept or decline the offer in follow-up writing.

⊃ Bar Incident

It's not a pretty sight—someone who has had too much to drink. But clear narration can move us from dry statistics to human realities.

1. The man slumps against the bar.
2. He is middle-aged.
3. He is a construction worker.
4. He wears his hard hat like a badge.
5. He slurps his drink.
6. It is his fifth of the evening.
7. His face is puffy.
8. His face is sun-weathered.
9. His face has started to show its age.
10. Age shows at the corners of his eyes.
11. His eyes are glassy and unfocused.
12. A tangled web of sounds surrounds him.
13. The sounds are loud voices.
14. The sounds are TV newscasters.
15. The sounds are country and western music.
16. A drunken grin spreads across his mouth.
17. It cracks through his depression.
18. He leans precariously to one side.
19. He begins to surrender to dizziness.
20. He then catches himself.
21. He mumbles aloud.

22. He repeats himself.
23. "Need a little sleep."
24. Then he wobbles to his feet.
25. He braces himself against the bar.
26. The bar is covered with glasses.
27. The glasses are stained and empty.
28. He stares at the young bartender.
29. The bartender is clearing away the debris.
30. The worker finishes off his drink.
31. The worker pushes his glass forward.
32. The worker demands "one for the road."
33. The bartender shakes his head no.
34. The bartender polishes the counter.
35. The counter is smooth and dark.
36. The bartender turns away.
37. Several seconds tick by.
38. The worker bristles in the mirror.
39. He clenches his fist around the glass.
40. His face darkens with blood.
41. His angry breathing quickens.

Invitation   Consider using this incident as an opener for "Alcohol Facts" in Unit 3. Or continue this story with follow-up writing.

⊃ *Water-Skier*

The sun is bright, and the air is warm. Light shimmers on the lake's rippled surface as the powerboat driver revs up the powerful engine.

1. The water-skier bobs in the water.
2. The water-skier looks like a yellow cork.
3. A life vest is bunched up near her ears.
4. Her muscles are tensed and ready.
5. The powerboat lurches forward.
6. The rope's slack suddenly tightens.
7. The water drags against her.
8. It is like a lover's embrace.
9. The embrace is smothering.
10. Suddenly she pulls herself up.

11. She is skimming its surface.
12. She is trying not to make any mistakes.
13. She leans lightly to one side.
14. She veers outward.
15. She crosses the boat's wake.
16. Then she dips back the other way.
17. She glides across a light chop.
18. A fine spray trails behind her.
19. It is silver in the afternoon sun.
20. Her hair flattens against her forehead.
21. She sways left and right like a dancer.
22. She glimpses her reflection on the water.
23. It looks like liquid glass.
24. It gleams beneath her skis.
25. It glitters beneath her skis.
26. Now she tightens her grip on the tow bar.
27. She lifts one ski slightly.
28. She leans against the boat's pull.
29. Her ski tip flicks a wave top.
30. It shatters her glassy reflection.
31. Then it is back better than ever.
32. Her hair is streaming behind her.
33. She finally signals "in."
34. The boat makes a wide turn.
35. It angles directly toward shore.
36. It then makes a sudden swerve.
37. The swerve takes it back to open water.
38. The skier holds on to the last moment.
39. Then she drops the rope.
40. She glides upright toward the beach.
41. She sinks slowly in the green water.
42. She feels the wash from the boat.
43. It laps against her back.
44. She slaps the water with her hand.
45. She shouts a whoop of joy.
46. "I did it."

Invitation   Using "Water-Skier" as a model, describe a challenge that gave you the fierce joy of real personal victory—a sense, perhaps, of having conquered your own fears.

⊃ *The Potter*

Making something from nothing—that's what we call "the creative process." Such magic can even happen with a simple lump of clay.

1. The potter hunches over his clay.
2. He adds drops of water to its surface.
3. The surface glistens beneath his fingers.
4. The gooey lump turns on the wheel.
5. The gooey lump is smoothed by hands.
6. The hands are slender and graceful.
7. The hands are always moving.
8. His brow wrinkles with concentration.
9. The clay becomes a slimy mess.
10. It is still solid.
11. It is now assuming liquid qualities.
12. He intends to shape these qualities.
13. He centers the soggy cone of clay.
14. It writhes against his fingertips.
15. His fingertips are carefully cupped.
16. He makes an indentation with his thumbs.
17. The clay begins to flatten.

18. It spreads against his palms.
19. He pushes slightly deeper.
20. Clay walls grow toward an overhead light.
21. He uses his thumbs and fingers.
22. His hands guide the clay's progress.
23. They shape it into a cylinder.
24. The cylinder is narrow at the base.
25. The cylinder widens toward the top.
26. One hand enters the turning shape.
27. The other pushes gently from the outside.
28. It leaves traces of fingertips.
29. The potter works the shape with care.
30. It broadens into an elegant bowl.
31. The bowl is thin-walled.
32. The bowl has a slightly curved lip.
33. The lip is like a child's pout.
34. The shape is now curved and magical.
35. The shape is beneath the potter's hands.
36. The shape responds to his slightest touch.
37. Finally the wheel slows to a stop.
38. The potter's face is smiling.
39. The potter's face is tranquil.
40. The wrinkles have momentarily vanished.
41. The wrinkles had creased his brow earlier.

Invitation   Like working with clay, the writer's work is also a creative process. Can you compare what you do in writing with the shaping described above? Describe how you see your creativity.

⊃ Coming Home

Has your home ever been burglarized or vandalized? If so, you probably know the feelings of disgust and anger: How come? Why me?

1. She stepped over a broken door.
2. She stepped through a doorway.
3. She came home to a cabin.

4. The cabin had one room.
5. Its interior was dark and musty.
6. There was a hole in the ceiling.
7. The hole was splintered.
8. Chimney stones had come through.
9. Dust danced in a shaft of sunlight.
10. Standing near the door was a stove.
11. The stove was a wood burner.
12. It had broken sections of stovepipe.
13. The stovepipe was covered with soot.
14. An old cupboard stood in the corner.
15. The glass was smashed from its doors.
16. Inside it were mismatched dishes.
17. Inside it were shattered mugs.
18. Inside it was a rock from the chimney.
19. Along the back wall was another hole.
20. The hole had once been a window.
21. Beneath it was a square table.
22. It had one leg kicked out.
23. Its top tilted downward.
24. Its top touched the floor.
25. A small iron bed was tipped over.
26. Its mattress was ripped open.
27. The mattress was gray and sagging.
28. Its stuffing was strewed everywhere.
29. She stared down at a wooden floor.
30. It was cracked and warped.
31. She wondered why someone had done this.
32. The cabin hadn't been much to begin with.
33. It was something she had helped build.
34. Now it was her inheritance to fix up.
35. First she'd have to deal with tears.

Invitation In follow-up writing, describe what you see as the root causes for senseless vandalism. Or, if you'd prefer, narrate the details of a time when you had a terrible surprise like this.

ↄ *American Pace*

The following piece of persuasive writing uses parallelism to drive home its point. For more on parallelism, see Appendix B.

1. Some people say something.
2. America is a desirable place to live.
3. It affords us basic freedoms.
4. The freedoms are unparalleled elsewhere.
5. Others argue something.
6. America is desirable.
7. Its living standard is very high.
8. This is compared with the standards of other nations.
9. The nations are highly industrialized.
10. Still others contend something.
11. America's desirability lies in its diversity.
12. The diversity is extraordinary.
13. The diversity is in people.
14. The diversity is in life-styles.
15. The diversity is in geography.
16. All of these statements may be true.
17. They ignore an erosion of community spirit.
18. The erosion seems to exist in many towns.
19. The erosion seems to exist in many cities.
20. We Americans have always been individualists.
21. Today's individualism is less generous.
22. Today's individualism is greedier.

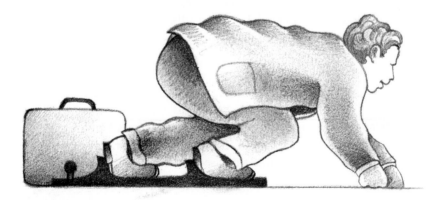

23. Many of us live at a frantic pace.
24. We careen like billiard balls through life.
25. Our handshakes are often obligatory.
26. Our handshakes are often hurried.
27. Our eyes flit from place to place.
28. They rarely pause for human contact.
29. Our talk is often silly and superficial.
30. Our talk is filled with clichés.
31. Our leisure is often spent on entertainment.
32. The entertainment is mindless.
33. The entertainment comes from TV dramas.
34. The entertainment comes from video stores.
35. The entertainment comes from music channels.
36. Our vacations are often a race.
37. The race is high-speed.
38. The race is from place to place.
39. Our vacations are not a spiritual renewal.
40. Our work is often something to be done with.
41. Our work is not a source of personal pride.
42. Our relationships are often mechanical.
43. Our relationships are often machine-stamped.
44. We assess what others can do for us.
45. Gone is the sense of real community.
46. Americans once shared this sense.

Invitation   Choose an approach for follow-up writing that responds to "American Pace": (1) discuss the *causes* of the problem, or (2) discuss your *solutions* to it.

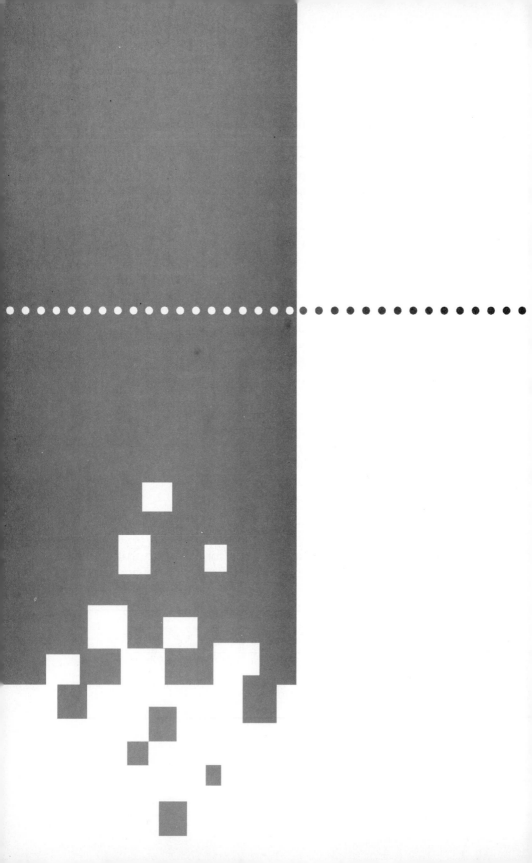

Recombining Practice

Most of us like to think of ourselves as individualists. In reality, however, much of what we learn comes from *imitating*, either consciously or unconsciously, what others do. We walk and talk and dress like those whom we admire, and we serve as apprentices to on-the-job coaches in schools, offices, and fast-food stores. Others show us how; we imitate.

What works in the world at large also works in writing. It was well over 2000 years ago that Greek and Roman teachers hit upon a powerful way to teach writing to students of that era. Extensive practice and immediate feedback were its key features. Students were asked to read and copy "model" writings of the day. Then they were told to *imitate* this exemplary prose.

We'll use a modern version of this time-proven method in Unit 5 activities. All exercises in this section derive from the work of skilled contemporary writers. Your first task is to do the combining as usual. Your second task is to compare your sentences with those of other students and with those provided by your instructor.

A WRITING APPRENTICESHIP

Think of Unit 5 exercises as an apprenticeship. The basic idea is to compare your style of writing with the style of various professionals. Sometimes you'll find similarities, sometimes not; but either way, you'll learn. The line-by-line comparison will teach you about the craft of writing by helping you understand your personal style of sentence construction.

This is *not* to say, of course, that the professional writer's sentences represent the "right answer" or the "best way" to combine a given set of sentences. In fact, with serious effort and the help of workshop partners, you may sometimes create sentences that are *superior* to the original ones. The point is that the original sentences are ones you can learn from, a standard against which you can measure your own efforts.

To illustrate what a recombining exercise looks like, here's a very brief example from *Survive the Savage Sea*, an exciting book by Dougal Robertson. The exercise opens with a bit of context to establish the scene. Please note that this exercise is unclustered (like the ones in Unit 4).

Context   *I had two large hooks left, and as I watched the long sleek shape of the sharks glide slowly by I resolved to keep them for another day.*

1.   One shark turned again.
2.   It cruised toward the dinghy.

3. Its speed was leisurely.
4. Its fin knifed the sea.
5. I grabbed the spear.
6. I struck savagely at its snout.
7. The shark went past the boat.
8. It flipped its tail wildly.
9. It was surprised.
10. It dived deep.
11. The other two cruised not far behind.
12. They kept a respectful distance.
13. I made the transit back to the raft.
14. I brought the fish.
15. The fish were newly caught.
16. The fish were for our lunch.

How would you capture the tension of this moment? Can you hear the sentences forming in your mind?

MAKING COMPARISONS

Let's now make sentence-by-sentence comparisons between two versions. After reading both paragraphs in their entirety, go back for a second look. Decide which version you prefer and why.

COMBINED VERSION. (1) Turning, one shark cruised toward the dinghy. (2) Its speed was leisurely; its fin knifed the sea. (3) As it went past the boat, I grabbed the spear and struck at its snout savagely. (4) The shark was surprised. (5) It flipped its tail wildly and dived deep. (6) The other two, cruising not far behind, kept a respectful distance while I made the transit back to the raft, bringing fish that were newly caught for our lunch.

ORIGINAL VERSION. [1] *One shark turned again and cruised at a leisurely speed toward the dinghy, its fin knifing the surface of the sea.* [2] *I grabbed the spear and struck savagely at its snout as it went past; the surprised shark flipped its tail wildly and dived deep, the two others cruising not far behind as I made the transit back to the raft with the newly caught fish for our lunch.*

One point of comparison is the number of sentences in the two versions. Do you favor more sentences—or fewer, longer ones? Try to find one sentence in each version that you especially like and one that you dislike.

Why do particular sentences either work or not work for you? Is it wording, sentence rhythm, or the "fit" in context?

When you find a sentence that you like, why not copy it into your notebook? Such a sentence might be the first one that Dougal Robertson writes. Notice how the absolute construction (*its fin knifing the surface of the sea*) provides the detail that brings the rest of the sentence to life. This is a sentence worth imitating. By doing so, you train yourself in sentence construction, adding to the skills that you can draw on later.

In working through the exercises in Unit 5, you will find some long sequences of sentences. Do not panic. Instead, think back to the combining you did in Unit 4, and approach the task slowly, deciding where to break a sequence into manageable clusters that you can combine in a meaningful way.

As always, remember that *sentence combining is an option, never a requirement.* You're the decision maker. [*Note:* The italized material within the Unit 5 selections is reprinted with the permission of the authors and publishers. Credits appear on page 235.]

⊃ *From* The Woman Warrior: Memoirs of a Childhood among Ghosts, *by Maxine Hong Kingston*

In her first year of American school, Maxine Ting Ting Hong spoke to no one and flunked kindergarten. From 5:00 to 7:30 p.m. each day, she also attended Chinese school, "where we chanted together, voices rising and falling, loud and soft." Her beautifully written memoir, *The Woman Warrior*, pulls together such experiences.

Directions Carefully read the context sentences below, listening to rhythm and pattern. Then combine sentences. Finally, compare your sentences with those of other students and with Maxine Hong Kingston's original text (provided by your instructor).

Context *Not all of the children who were silent at American school found voice in Chinese school. One new teacher said each of us had to get up and recite in front of the class, who was to listen. My sister and I had memorized the lesson* *perfectly. We said it to each other at home, one chanting, one listening. The teacher called on my sister to recite first. It was the first time a teacher had called on the second-born to go first.*

1. My sister was scared.
2. She glanced at me.
3. She looked away.
4. I looked down at my desk.
5. I hoped that she could do it.
6. If she could, then I would have to.
7. She opened her mouth.
8. A voice came out.
9. It wasn't a whisper.
10. It wasn't a proper voice either.
11. I hoped that she would not cry.
12. The fear would break up her voice.
13. It would be like twigs underfoot.

She sounded as if she were trying to sing through weeping or strangling.

14. She did not pause to end the embarrassment.
15. She did not stop to end the embarrassment.
16. She kept going.
17. She said the last word.
18. Then she sat down.
19. It was my turn.
20. The same voice came out.
21. It was a crippled animal.
22. The animal was running on broken legs.
23. You could hear the splinter in my voice.
24. It was like bones rubbing jagged against each other.
25. I was loud, though.
26. I was glad I didn't whisper.
27. There was one little girl.
28. The girl whispered.

Invitation Do you recall, like Maxine Hong Kingston, a school experience where you felt embarrassed to speak up? Create the scene and situation for the reader. What did you learn from it?

⊃ *From* A Summer Life, *by Gary Soto*

Growing up Hispanic in California provided Gary Soto with much to write about as an adult. The short personal narratives in *A Summer Life* capture his boyhood and adolescent experiences in beautifully crafted prose. In addition to his essays, Soto also writes award-winning fiction and poetry. Here he sets off on a bike ride.

Directions Carefully read the context sentences below, listening to rhythm and pattern. Then combine sentences. Finally, compare your sentences with those of other students and with Gary Soto's original text (provided by your instructor).

Context *Roeding Park was five miles from home, far enough for me to act goofy and spit the shells of sunflower seeds during a hard-pedaling bike ride. A shell stuck to my cheek before the wind ripped it off. I let the one on my forehead stay until I got off my bike, sweaty and tired, and walked to the pond where black kids in collarless T-shirts fished.*

1. I stopped to watch them awhile.
2. I cautiously held on to my bike.
3. I was afraid one of them might throw down his pole.
4. He might pedal off with what was mine.
5. The pond was shaped like a kidney.
6. It rippled with mosquitoes.
7. It rippled with water skeeters.
8. Paper cups floated near the edges.
9. Ice cream wrappers floated near the edges.
10. I left and climbed a Sherman tank.
11. The tank was painted with gold.
12. It was also littered with paper cups.
13. It was also littered with wrappers.
14. The turret was slashed with initials.
15. The turret was slashed with dumb faces.
16. The sun was already above the trees.
17. The sun was yellow as a tooth.
18. The shadows were leaning west instead of east.

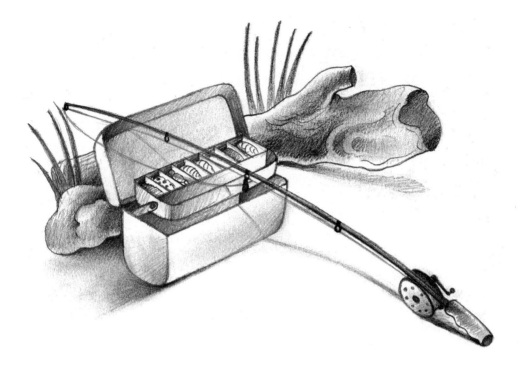

19. The shadows lean east when the sun goes down.
20. It was a weekday.
21. Some families were banging folding chairs.
22. The chairs were from station wagons.
23. The chairs were aluminum.
24. One man was carrying an ice chest on his shoulder.
25. A couple was smoothing an army blanket.
26. They placed heavy objects at each corner.
27. The objects were a purse.
28. The objects were an ice chest.
29. The objects were two soft tennis shoes.
30. This was so the wind would not peel it back.

Invitation Do you remember childhood adventures as clearly as Gary Soto? Think back to one where you tested the limits that had been set for you. What did you learn from this experience?

⊃ *From* Desert Exile: The Uprooting of a Japanese American Family, *by Yoshiko Uchida*

Yoshiko Uchida was a happy, successful college student in the early 1940s—on her way toward becoming an award-winning writer. But then came Pearl Harbor and the federal government's decision to move 110,000 persons of Japanese ancestry into detention camps, without charges or trial. Yoshiko Uchida was part of the herd.

Directions   Carefully read the context sentences below, listening to rhythm and pattern. Then combine sentences. Finally, compare your sentences with those of other students and with Yoshiko Uchida's original text (provided by your instructor).

Context   *Barrack 16 was not a barrack at all, but a long stable raised a few feet off the ground with a broad ramp the horses had used to reach their stalls. Each stall was now numbered and ours was number 40. That the stalls should have been called "apartments" was a euphemism so ludicrous it was comical.*

1. We reached stall number 40.
2. We pushed open the narrow door.
3. We looked uneasily into the vacant darkness.
4. The stall was about ten by twenty feet.
5. It was empty except for three Army cots.
6. The cots were folded.
7. The cots were lying on the floor.
8. Dust covered the linoleum.
9. Dirt covered the linoleum.
10. Wood shavings covered the linoleum.
11. The linoleum had been laid over boards.
12. The boards were covered with manure.
13. The smell of horses hung in the air.
14. The corpses of many insects still clung to the walls.
15. The corpses were whitened.

16. The walls had been hastily white-washed.
17. High on either side of the entrance were two windows.
18. The windows were small.
19. They were our only source of daylight.
20. The stall was divided into sections by Dutch doors.
21. The doors were worn down by teeth marks.
22. Each stall was separated from the adjoining one.
23. The separation was only by rough partitions.
24. The partitions stopped a foot short of the roof.
25. The roof was sloping.
26. That space deprived us of all but visual privacy.
27. It was perhaps a good source of ventilation for horses.
28. We couldn't even be sure of visual privacy.
29. There were crevices in the dividing walls.
30. There were knotholes in the dividing walls.

Invitation   Have you ever had to live in a terrible place? One way to gain power over such memories—to put them behind you—is through writing. Describe the place that you disliked so much.

➲ *From* Growing Up, *by Russell Baker*

In 1983, Russell Baker won the Pulitzer prize for biography. With many years of solid experience as a journalist, Baker writes in a clear, direct style, without indulging in self-pity, about growing up poor. Here he describes his mother's positive efforts to make Christmas memorable and joyous, even on a welfare budget.

Directions   Carefully read the context sentences below, listening to rhythm and pattern. Then combine sentences. Finally, compare your sentences with those of other students and with Russell Baker's original text (provided by your instructor).

Context *Christmas was the one occasion on which my mother surrendered to unabashed sentimentality. A week beforehand she always concocted homemade root beer, sealed it in canning jars, and stored it in the bathroom for the yeast to ferment. Now and then, sitting in the adjoining kitchen, we heard a loud thump from the bathroom and knew that one of the jars had exploded, but she always made enough to allow for breakage.*

1. She took girlish delight.
2. Her delight was in keeping gifts hidden.
3. The gifts were brightly wrapped.
4. They were hidden in closets.
5. She spent Christmas Eve in frenzies of baking.
6. She baked cakes.
7. She baked pies.
8. She baked gingerbread cookies.
9. They were cut and decorated.
10. They looked like miniature brown pine trees.
11. They looked like miniature brown Santa Clauses.

12. She took Doris and me to the street corner.
13. This was in the afternoon.
14. There trees were piled high.
15. She searched through them.
16. She found one that satisfied our taste.
17. Our taste was for symmetry.
18. Our taste was for fullness.
19. It was my job to set the tree up in the parlor.
20. It was Doris's job to set the tree up in the parlor.
21. We were to weight it down with ornaments.
22. We were to weight it down with lights.
23. We were to weight it down with silver icicles.
24. She prepared Christmas Eve dinner.
25. This was a ritual meal.
26. Its centerpiece was oysters.
27. She disliked oysters.
28. She always ate them on Christmas Eve.
29. Oysters were the centerpiece of the traditional supper.
30. The supper was for Christmas Eve.
31. She remembered it from her girlhood.
32. Her girlhood was in Virginia.
33. She served them.
34. She perpetuated the customs of Papa's household.

Invitation Celebrations and rituals—like Christmas, Yom Kippur, birthdays, Thanksgiving—probably stand out in your mind. Describe one of these with the clarity you see in Russell Baker's writing.

⊃ *From* An American Childhood, *by Annie Dillard*

As a kid in Pittsburgh, Annie Dillard was curious about almost everything —geography, birds and rocks and insects, drawing. "Things snagged me," she writes. She visited museums, read voraciously, and observed the world around here. Watching a Polyphemus moth, for example, made a searing impression on her.

Directions Carefully read the context sentences below, listening to rhythm and pattern. Then combine sentences. Finally, compare your sentences with those of other students and with Annie Dillard's original text (provided by your instructor).

Context *The mason jar sat on the teacher's desk; the big moth emerged inside it. The moth had clawed a hole in its hot cocoon and crawled out, as if agonizingly, over the course of an hour, one leg at a time; we children watched around the desk, transfixed. After it emerged, the wet, mashed thing turned around walking on the jar's green bottom, then painstakingly climbed the twig with which the jar was furnished.*

1. The moth was there at the twig's top.
2. The moth shook its clumps of wings.
3. The wings were sodden.
4. It spread those wings.
5. The wings were beautiful.
6. Blood would fill their veins.
7. The birth fluids would harden.
8. The birth fluids were on the wings' frail sheets.
9. Hardening would make them tough as sails.
10. But the moth could not spread its wings at all.
11. The jar was too small.
12. The wings could not fill.
13. They hardened.
14. They were still crumpled from the cocoon.

A smaller moth could have spread its wings to their utmost in that mason jar, but the Polyphemus moth was big.

15. Its gold furred body was almost as big as a mouse.
16. Its wings would have extended six inches.
17. Its wings were brown, yellow, pink, and blue.
18. The extension was tip to tip.
19. This was if there had been no mason jar.
20. It would have been as big as a wren.
21. The teacher let the creature go.
22. The creature was deformed.
23. We all left the classroom.
24. We paraded out behind the teacher.
25. Our parade was with pomp and circumstance.

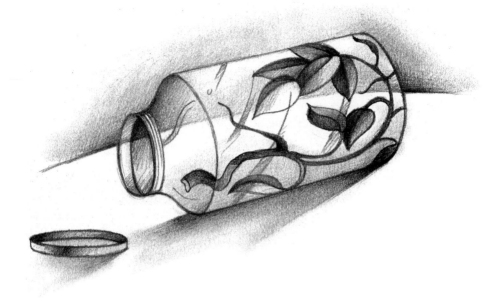

26. She bounced the moth from the jar.
27. She set it on the school's driveway.
28. The moth set out walking.
29. It could only heave the clumps.
30. The clumps were golden and wrinkly.
31. The clumps were where its wings would have been.
32. It could only crawl down the school driveway.
33. Crawling was on its six frail legs.
34. The moth crawled down the driveway.
35. It headed toward the rest of Shadyside.
36. This was an area of fine houses.
37. This was an area of expensive apartments.
38. This was an area of fashionable shops.

Invitation Like Annie Dillard, you may have strong nightmarish memories from childhood. Record such a memory as fully as you can, and discuss what it reveals about you—its personal meaning.

↺ *From* Strawberry Road, *by Yoshimi Ishikawa*

Sitting on a Los Angeles pier after immigrating from Japan to America, Yoshimi Ishikawa felt "absolutely lost." Not long after, however, he began to learn about America from "the ground up"—working as a farm laborer in California's strawberry fields. He also took courses in an American high school to learn English.

Directions Carefully read the context sentences below, listening to rhythm and pattern. Then combine sentences. Finally, compare your sentences with those of other students and with Yoshimi Ishikawa's original text (provided by your instructor).

Context *Speech and drama was my only final. The test consisted of reciting a dramatic passage or famous political speech. Talking for five minutes in front of an audience was no easy feat—especially in English. I wanted, however, to repay the kindness of my teacher, and I worked on my speech for days. I had chosen John F. Kennedy's inaugural speech, but, no matter how hard I tried, I couldn't get past the third line. Whenever I tried to memorize a few more of the lines, I would forget what I had already learned. In spite of this, I prepared assiduously for the final, which would take place in the school auditorium.* (From STRAWBERRY ROAD by Yoshimi Ishikawa translated by Eve Zimmerman, published by Kodansha International Ltd. Copyright © 1991 by Yoshimi Ishikama. Reprinted by permission. All rights reserved.)

1. Americans must be able to express themselves.
2. This class was good preparation for life.
3. The basic philosophy seems simple enough.
4. Make sure others listen to you.
5. This is before you listen to them.
6. It is a key to how America was formed by people.
7. The people spoke such different languages.
8. Unity comes about much more speedily.
9. You force your way of thinking upon others.
10. You make them listen to you.
11. This is something at which Anglo-Saxons excel.
12. America makes an impression on foreigners.
13. The impression is violent.
14. This is a result not just of its high crime rate.
15. This is a result of the nature of conversation here.

16. The conversation is one-sided.
17. The power to persuade is a weapon.
18. The power to be eloquent is a weapon.
19. One needs weapons to survive in America.
20. Therefore, every high school has facilities.
21. The high schools are American.
22. The facilities are for public speaking.
23. The exam began.
24. The students got up onstage one by one.
25. They recited speeches or soliloquies.
26. These were from famous plays.
27. I felt bewitched by the power of English speech.
28. One of the students recited a speech by Hamlet.
29. The student was less bright.
30. He sounded superb.
31. Exclamations arose from the audience.
32. Our teacher was taking notes.
33. She was at the foot of the stage.
34. Finally it was my turn.

Invitation What kinds of formal or informal "tests" have you faced—in school, on the street, or at work? Describe the occasion of a particularly memorable challenge and its outcome.

⊃ *From* I Know Why the Caged Bird Sings, *by Maya Angelou*

Afro-American writer Maya Angelou has authored several best-selling autobiographies and collections of poetry. She took the country by storm with her first book, which depicted her childhood memories up through high school graduation. In this excerpt, she hits the California streets with three dollars and no place to sleep.

Directions Carefully read the context sentences below, listening to rhythm and pattern. Then combine sentences. Finally, compare your sentences with those of other students and with Maya Angelou's original text (provided by your instructor).

Context   *I spent the day wandering aimlessly through the bright streets. The noisy penny arcades with their gaggle-giggle of sailors and children were tempting, but after walking through one of them it was obvious that I could only win more chances and no money. I went to the library and used part of my day reading science fiction, and in its marble washroom I changed my bandage.*

1. I passed a junkyard on one flat street.
2. It was littered with the carcasses of old cars.
3. The dead hulks were somehow so uninviting.
4. I decided to inspect them.

5. I wound my way through the discards.
6. A temporary situation sprang to mind.
7. I would find a clean or cleanish car.
8. I would spend the night in it.
9. I had the optimism of ignorance.
10. I thought something.
11. The morning was bound to bring a solution.
12. The solution would be more pleasant.
13. A gray car caught my eye.
14. It was tall-bodied.
15. It was near the fence.
16. Its seats were untorn.
17. It had no rims or wheels.
18. It sat evenly on its fenders.
19. The idea bolstered my sense of freedom.
20. The idea was sleeping in the near open.
21. I was a loose kite in a gentle wind.
22. I was floating.
23. I had only my will for an anchor.
24. I decided upon the car.
25. I got inside it.
26. I ate the tuna sandwiches.
27. I then searched the floorboards for holes.
28. Something was more alarming than the shadowed hulks.
29. The hulks were in the junkyard.
30. Something was more alarming than the night.
31. The night was quickly descending.
32. This was the fear that rats might scurry in.
33. They might eat off my nose as I slept.
34. Some cases had been recently reported in the papers.
35. My gray choice, however, seemed rat-tight.
36. I abandoned my idea of taking another walk.
37. I decided to sit steady.
38. I decided to wait for sleep.

Invitation Did you ever run away from home or challenge parental authority in some dramatic way? In writing, recall the situation and how you dealt with it. What did you learn from the experience?

⊃ *From* Blue Highways: A Journey into America, *by William Least Heat Moon*

"On the old highway maps of America," writes William Least Heat Moon, "the main routes were red and the back roads blue." After the breakup of his marriage—what he calls the "Indian Wars"—he took to the back roads in an old Ford van ("Ghost Dancing") for an around-the-country trip. The journal he kept led to a best-seller.

Directions   Carefully read the context sentences below, listening to rhythm and pattern. Then combine sentences. Finally, compare your sentences with those of other students and with William Least Heat Moon's original text (provided by your instructor).

Context   *Because the Navajo prefer widely dispersed clusters of clans to village life, I'd seen nothing resembling a hamlet for seventy-five miles. But Hopi Polacca almost looked like a Western town in spite of the Indian ways here and there: next to a floral-print bedsheet on a clothesline hung a coyote skin, and beside box houses were adobe bread ovens shaped like skep beehives. The Navajo held to his hogan, the Hopi his oven. Those things persisted.*

1. Three mesas were like bony fingers.
2. Three mesas reached down from larger Black Mesa.
3. They reached into the middle of Hopi land.
4. Something was true not long ago.
5. The only way onto these mesas was by handholds.
6. The handholds were in the steep rock heights.
7. The Hopi look out upon a thousand square miles.
8. This is from the tops of the mesas.
9. Second Mesa was at the heart of the reservation.
10. The heart was topographic.
11. The heart was cultural.
12. Something is traditional for Hopis.
13. Hopis prefer to live on precipices.
14. This is like the eagles they hold sacred.
15. The Hopi Cultural Center was built there.
16. It was not far from the edge of Second Mesa.

In the gallery were drawings of mythic figures by Hopi children who fused centuries and cultures with grotesque Mudhead Kachinas wearing large terra-cotta masks and jackolantern smiles, dancing atop spaceships with Darth Vader and Artoo Deetoo.

17. I ate *nokquivi* at the Center.
18. It was a good hominy stew with baked chile peppers.
19. I had no luck in striking up a conversation.
20. I drove on toward the western edge of the mesa.
21. Not far from the tribal garage stood small houses.
22. The houses were built of sandstone.
23. The garage was for TRIBAL VEHICLES ONLY.
24. Their sandstone slabs were precisely cut.
25. Their sandstone slabs were precisely fitted.
26. It was as if done by ancient Aztecs.
27. The Aztecs are a people related to the Hopi.
28. The solid houses blended with the tawny land so well.
29. They appeared to be part of the living rock.
30. All were empty.
31. The residents had moved to prefabs.
32. The residents had moved to doublewides.

Invitation William Least Heat Moon is a keen observer of the world around him. Describe a scene—from childhood, from your neighborhood, from across campus—so that your reader can see it.

⊃ *From* Two-Part Invention: The Story of a Marriage, *by Madeleine L'Engle*

As the award-winning author of over thirty books, Madeleine L'Engle has a writer's eye for detail, even when that detail is painful to record. In her 1988 memoir, she describes a hospital vigil, where she watches her husband's deteriorating health. In the crisis below, her husband suffers from a collapsed lung, with surgery imminent.

Directions Carefully read the context sentences below, listening to rhythm and pattern. Then combine sentences. Finally, compare your sentences with those of other students and with Madeleine L'Engle's original text (provided by your instructor).

Context *The young general surgeon comes in. Amazingly, I am allowed to stay in the room, to hold Hugh's hand. It is explained that a tube will have to be put between the ribs and into the chest so that the invasive air will be sucked out. The tube will have to stay in place until after the surgery.*

1. The surgeon prepares.
2. He dons surgical gloves.
3. A nurse is with him.
4. She is to hand him the local anesthetic.
5. She is to hand him sterile fluid.
6. She is ultimately to hand him the scalpel.
7. I stand at the head of the bed.
8. There I can clasp Hugh's hand.
9. He can hold hard.
10. This is when the pain is bad.
11. He is given several shots of local anesthetic.
12. Then the surgeon takes a small scalpel.
13. The surgeon makes an incision.
14. The incision is a little over an inch long.
15. It is just above the ribs.
16. Then he tells Hugh something.
17. What is coming next is going to hurt.
18. He will hear a great whoosh of air.
19. The surgeon puts his fingers in the incision.
20. He feels for the right place.
21. Then the tube is thrust in.
22. Air does indeed whoosh out.
23. Hugh almost screams with pain.
24. But the tube is in.
25. The incision is sewn up.
26. There is a plastic tank.
27. It is hung at the side of the bed.
28. "You will sound like an aquarium," the surgeon says.
29. Hugh does sound like one.
30. He is exhausted.
31. He is in pain.

Invitation Caring for a loved one is often a deeply emotional experience. Can you recall doing this or visiting a hospital where someone was being treated? Write about the scene that moved you.

⊃ *From* Starting from Home: A Writer's Beginnings, *by Milton Meltzer*

With over seventy books to his credit—many on social issues such as poverty, slavery, and women's rights—Milton Meltzer is no stranger to writing. In his memoir, he describes experiences that shaped his life. One of these occurred just before his older brother Allan ran away from home at age 14 to work in New York City.

Directions Carefully read the context sentences below, listening to rhythm and pattern. Then combine sentences. Finally, compare your sentences with those of other students and with Milton Meltzer's original text (provided by your instructor).

Context *With nearly four years separating us, we [Allan and I] didn't play together or share friends. Smart-ass kid that he was, he wanted desperately to be accepted by the bigger boys in class. After school, he chose the toughest kids in the neighborhood to hang out with. They didn't care for school, so neither did he. He sassed the teachers and broke most of the rules. Suspended twice, he became the constant worry of Ma and Pa. They knew how intelligent he was, and they hoped that somehow they would be able to send their first-born to college. With that big mouth, they used to say smilingly, you can be a fine lawyer some day. . . .*

1. He reached Classical.
2. It was the Worcester high school.
3. It was designed to prepare students for college.
4. Something happened in his first year there.
5. He missed class for a while.
6. He was recovering from a broken leg.

7. It was broken during a football game.
8. The game was in the neighborhood.
9. He got back to school.
10. He didn't work hard to catch up in math.
11. Mr. Howland gave him a "D warning."
12. That meant something.
13. He had to stay in after school each day.
14. He had to study under supervision.
15. Mr. Howland came up behind him one afternoon.
16. Mr. Howland saw that Allan was reading a novel.
17. It was hidden between the pages of a math text.
18. The math text was propped up on his desk.
19. He snatched it away.
20. He said something angrily.
21. "Meltzer, you're a thief!"
22. Allan was shocked by such a charge.
23. Allan said, "What do you mean by that?"
24. The teacher made a reply.
25. "You're stealing the school's time!"
26. Allan gave Mr. Howland a shove.
27. The teacher fell over a chair.
28. Allan ran out of the room.
29. Something happened the next day.
30. He entered the school.
31. The principal was waiting for him.
32. The principal was Mr. Fenner.
33. "Get out!" he yelled.
34. "You're expelled!"

Invitation   Do you recall a dramatic incident in school between a teacher and a student (perhaps you yourself)? What circumstances surrounded this incident? Write about this event and its meaning.

⊃ From The Joy Luck Club, by Amy Tan

Chinese-American writer Amy Tan achieved wide recognition in 1989 with the publication of *The Joy Luck Club*, her first book. With clarity and style, Tan's book depicts the lives and values of Chinese-American mothers and daughters. More broadly, it deals with the tensions between generations that concern us all.

Directions Carefully read the context sentences below, listening to rhythm and pattern. Then combine sentences. Finally, compare your sentences with those of other students and with Amy Tan's original text (provided by your instructor).

Context *My mother started the San Francisco version of the Joy Luck Club in 1949, two years before I was born. This was the year my mother and father left China with one stiff leather trunk filled only with fancy silk dresses. There was no time to pack anything else, my mother had explained to my father after they boarded the boat. Still his hands swam frantically between the slippery silks, looking for his cotton shirts and wool pants.*

1. They arrived in San Francisco.
2. My father made her hide those shiny clothes.
3. She wore the same brown-checked Chinese dress.
4. This was until something happened.
5. The Refugee Welcome Society gave her two dresses.
6. The dresses were hand-me-downs.
7. They were all too large.
8. They were in sizes for American women.
9. The society was composed of a group of ladies.
10. The ladies were American missionaries.
11. They were white-haired.
12. They came from the First Chinese Baptist Church.
13. And my parents could not refuse their invitation.
14. The invitation was to join the church.
15. This was because of the gifts.
16. Nor could they ignore the old ladies' advice.
17. The advice was practical.
18. The advice was to improve their English.
19. The improvement was through Bible study class.
20. The class was on Wednesday nights.
21. Later the improvement was through choir practice.
22. The practice was on Saturday mornings.
23. This was how my parents met the Hsus.
24. This was how my parents met the Jongs.

25. This was how my parents met the St. Clairs.
26. My mother could sense something.
27. The women of these families also had tragedies.
28. The tragedies were unspeakable.
29. They had left the tragedies behind in China.
30. The women also had hopes.
31. They couldn't begin to express hopes in their English.
32. Their English was fragile.
33. Or at least, my mother recognized the numbness.
34. The numbness was in these women's faces.
35. And she saw how quickly their eyes moved.
36. She told them her idea.
37. Her idea was for the Joy Luck Club.

Invitation What events are part of your family's history? Recall a story that you have been told by parents, relatives, or siblings about your family. Why is this story important to you now?

ↄ *From* Et Cetera, Et Cetera: Notes of a Word-Watcher, *by Lewis Thomas*

Some people have narrow, specialized interests. Not Lewis Thomas. Internationally known for his work as a physician and medical researcher, Thomas has also been praised for his excellent science writing. One of his recent books grows out of a lifelong love affair with language. Here he discusses animal communication.

Directions   Carefully read the context sentences below, listening to rhythm and pattern. Then combine sentences. Finally, compare your sentences with those of other students and with Lewis Thomas's original text (provided by your instructor).

Context   *Other creatures have ways of communicating with each other, sending clear and explicit messages, but never with the subtlety and complexity of human speech. But perhaps some of the messages represent the rudiments of language; perhaps the gift of something like speech has been selected for in the evolution of all species and only we humans, thus far, have broken through and emerged with metaphor as our sign of triumph.*

1. Dolphins make sounds.
2. The sounds seem to be messages.
3. The messages are beyond our comprehension.
4. Whales sing songs to each other.
5. Whales sing across undersea miles.
6. The songs are deep and mysterious.
7. Fireflies congregate by the millions.
8. The congregation is in tropical trees.
9. They flash together in absolute synchrony.
10. The flashing marks the species ready for mating.
11. Crickets chirp in tight rhythms.
12. Each chirp identifies family members.
13. The family members are keeping in touch.
14. Something happens when the weather chills down.
15. The male crickets chirp at a slower rate.
16. The chirping is done so predictably.

17. Farmers can make guesses at the temperature change.
18. Naturalists can make guesses at the temperature change.
19. The guesses are accurate.
20. It is a comfort to know something.
21. The female's receptor apparatus accommodates.
22. The apparatus slows accordingly.
23. Sometimes the messages are sent across species lines.
24. The honeyguide is a small African bird.
25. It locates honeybee hives.
26. The hives are in forest trees.
27. It signals the exact location to human beings.
28. It signals by a specialized call.
29. The call is seemingly deliberate.
30. The human beings follow the bird.
31. The human beings then break open the hives.
32. The human beings leave behind ample supplies.
33. The supplies are for the birds' needs.

Invitation   Have you ever cared for an animal with whom you shared the "rudiments of language"? Describe this animal and the type of communication, or love, that evolved between the two of you.

⊃ *From* The Story of My Life, *by Helen Keller*

When Helen Keller was nineteen months old, she was struck down by an illness that left her deaf and blind. She languished in a dark, silent world until a remarkable teacher, Annie Sullivan, helped her begin to acquire the rudiments of language with "finger-writing." Helen Keller's story has inspired millions of handicapped people.

Directions   Carefully read the context sentences below, listening to rhythm and pattern. Then combine sentences. Finally, compare your sentences with those of other students and with Helen Keller's original text (provided by your instructor).

Context *One day, while I was playing with my new [ceramic] doll, Miss Sullivan put my big rag doll into my lap also, spelled "d-o-l-l" and tried to make me understand that "d-o-l-l" applied to both. Earlier in the day we had had a tussle over the words "m-u-g" and "w-a-t-e-r." Miss Sullivan had tried to impress it upon me that "m-u-g" is mug and that "w-a-t-e-r" is water, but I persisted in confounding the two. . . .*

1. We walked down the path to the well-house.
2. We were attracted by the fragrance of honeysuckle.
3. Honeysuckle covered the well-house.
4. Someone was drawing water.
5. My teacher placed my hand under the spout.
6. The cool stream gushed over one hand.
7. She spelled into the other the word *water*.
8. First she did this slowly.
9. Then she did this rapidly.
10. I stood still.
11. My whole attention was fixed upon the motions.

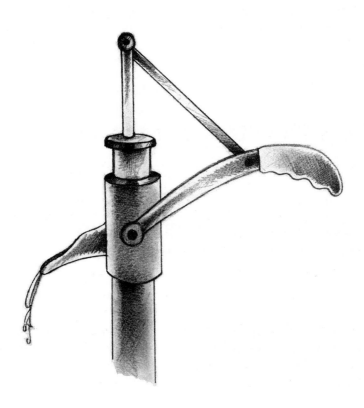

12. Her fingers made the motions.
13. Something happened suddenly.
14. I felt a misty consciousness.
15. It was like something forgotten.
16. It was a thrill of returning thought.
17. Somehow the mystery of language was revealed to me.
18. I knew something then.
19. "W-a-t-e-r" meant the wonderful cool something.
20. It was flowing over my hand.
21. The living word awakened my soul.
22. It gave my soul light.
23. It gave my soul hope.
24. It gave my soul joy.
25. It set my soul free.
26. It is true that there were still barriers.
27. The barriers could in time be swept away.
28. I left the well-house eager to learn.
29. Everything had a name.
30. Each name gave birth to a new thought.
31. We returned to the house.
32. Every object seemed to quiver with life.
33. I touched every object.

Invitation   Have you ever had a "breakthrough" like that experienced by Helen Keller? Describe a time when you felt the joy of success, learning, or personal recognition.

⊃ *From* A River Runs Through It,
by Norman Maclean

Perhaps you've seen Robert Redford's film of Norman Maclean's *A River Runs Through It*. If so, you already know the dramatic Montana setting for the story of Norman Maclean's family and his interest in fly-fishing. The following passage records the last time that Norman fishes with his father and his brother Paul.

Directions Carefully read the context sentences below, listening to rhythm and pattern. Then combine sentences. Finally, compare your sentences with those of other students and with Norman Maclean's original text (provided by your instructor).

Context *Paul was startled for only a moment. Then he spotted Father on the bank rubbing his shoulder, and Paul laughed, shook his fist at him, backed to shore and went downstream to get out of rock range. From there he waded into the water again, but now he was far enough away so that we couldn't see his line or loops. He was a man with a wand in a river, and whatever happened we had to guess from what the man and the wand and the river did.*

1. He waded out.
2. His big right arm swung back and forth.
3. Each circle of his arm inflated his chest.
4. Each circle was faster.
5. Each circle was higher.
6. Each circle was longer.
7. His arm became defiant.
8. His chest breasted the sky.
9. We could see no line on shore.
10. We were sure of something.
11. The air above him was singing with loops of line.
12. The loops never touched the water.
13. Each time they passed and sang.
14. They got bigger and bigger.
15. And we knew what was in his mind.
16. We watched the lengthening defiance of his arm.
17. He was not going to let his fly touch any water.
18. The water was close to shore.
19. The small fish were there.
20. The middle-sized fish were there.

We knew from his arm and chest that all parts of him were saying, "No small one for the last one."

21. Everything was going into one big cast.
22. The cast was for one last big fish.
23. Our angle was high on the bank.
24. My father and I could see something in the distance.

25. The wand was not going to let the fly touch the water.
26. A rock iceberg was in the middle of the river.
27. Just its tip was exposed above the water.
28. Underneath it was a big rock house.
29. It met all the residential requirements for big fish.
30. There was powerful water.
31. The water carried food to the front and back doors.
32. There was rest behind the doors.
33. There was shade behind the doors.

My father said, "There has to be a big one out there."

Invitation   Recall a vivid scene from your personal history—one that captures a memory that you value. Narrate what happens, and tell why this scene is important to you.

⊃ *From* Lakota Woman, *by Mary Crow Dog and Richard Erdoes*

....

"I am a woman of the Red Nation, a Sioux woman," writes Mary Crow Dog, who grew up fatherless on the Rosebud Reservation in South Dakota, in a one-room cabin without electricity or running water. At an early age she learned about whippings at school, alcohol, racism, and rape. And yet there were also positive influences.

Directions   Carefully read the context sentences below, listening to rhythm and pattern. Then combine sentences. Finally, compare your sentences with those of other students and with Mary Crow Dog's original text (provided by your instructor).

Context   *One woman, Elsie Flood, a niece of Grandma's, had a big influence upon me. She was a turtle woman, a strong, self-reliant person, because a turtle stands for strength, resolution, and long life. A turtle heart beats and beats for days, long after the turtle itself is dead. It keeps on beating all by itself. In* *traditional families a beaded charm in the shape of a turtle is fastened to a newborn child's cradle. The baby's navel cord is put inside this turtle charm, which is believed to protect the infant from harm and bad spirits. The charm is also supposed to make the child live to a great old age. A turtle is a strength of mind, a communication with the thunder.*

1. I loved to visit Aunt Elsie.
2. This was to listen to her stories.
3. She looked like Grandma.
4. Grandma had high cheekbones.
5. She had a voice like water.
6. The water was bubbling.
7. Her talking was with a deep sound.
8. Her talking was with a throaty sound.
9. And she talked fast.
10. She mixed Indian and English together.
11. I had to pay strict attention.
12. I wanted to understand what she told me.
13. She always paid her bills.
14. She earned a living by her arts and crafts.
15. This was her beautiful work with beads.
16. This was her beautiful work with porcupine quills.
17. This is what she called her "Indian novelties."
18. She was also a medicine woman.

19. She was an old-time woman.
20. She was carrying her pack on her back.
21. She would not let a man carry her burden.
22. She could not let a younger woman carry her burden.
23. She carried it herself.
24. She did not ask for help from anybody.
25. She did not accept help from anybody.
26. She was proud of her turtle strength.
27. She used turtles as her protection.

Wherever she went, she always had some little live turtles with her and all kinds of things made out of tortoiseshell, little charms and boxes.

28. She had a little place in Martin.
29. It was halfway between Rosebud and Pine Ridge.
30. There she lived alone.
31. She was very independent.
32. She was always glad to have me visit her.
33. Once she came to our home.
34. She was trudging along as usual.
35. She had the heavy pack on her back.
36. She had two shopping bags.
37. They were full of herbs and strange things.
38. She also brought a present for me.
39. The present was two turtles.
40. They were tiny and very lively.
41. She had painted Indian designs.
42. The designs were on their shells and bottoms.
43. She communicated with them by name.
44. One she called "Come."
45. The other she called "Go."
46. They always waddled over to her.
47. She called to them to get their food.
48. She had a special kind of feed for them.
49. She would leave me whole bags of it.
50. These small twin turtles stayed tiny.
51. They never grew.
52. One day the white principal's son came over.
53. He smashed them.
54. He simply stomped them to death.
55. My aunt heard it.
56. She said that this was an evil sign for her.

Invitation   Is there an adult, like Aunt Elsie, who had a positive influence on your development as a child? Describe that person and how he or she helped shape your character.

⊃ *From* Papa, My Father, *by Leo Buscaglia*

A celebrated teacher, writer, and public speaker, Leo Buscaglia is well known for his views about love. Many of his lessons came from memorable experiences with his father, an Italian immigrant with a fifth-grade education. In this richly narrated excerpt, Buscaglia describes the work of making wine with his father.

Directions   Carefully read the context sentences below, listening to rhythm and pattern. Then combine sentences. Finally, compare your sentences with those of other students and with Leo Buscaglia's original text (provided by your instructor).

Context   *When I was growing up, we had many festivities in our home. None, except Christmas and Easter, topped the one night a year that we made new wine. The anticipation and preparation began in July and August, long before the eventful September evening when the truckload of grapes was delivered. By then Papa had made several visits to his friends—grape growers in Cucamonga, about forty miles from our home—to observe the progress of his grapes. He had spent hours scouring the barrels in which wine would be made and stored, and applying antirust varnish on every visible metal part of the wine-making equipment. The fermenting vat had been filled with water to swell the wood.*

1. Something happened on the appointed evening.
2. The truck would arrive after nightfall.
3. It was brimming with small Cabernet grapes.
4. They were tough-skinned.
5. They were sweet-smelling.

6. The boxes of grapes were hand-carried.
7. It was about two hundred feet to the garage.
8. A giant empty vat awaited there.
9. A crusher was positioned on top of the vat.
10. The crusher was hand-powered.
11. Its positioning was precarious.
12. It was ready to grind noisily into the night.
13. Thousands of grapes were poured into it.
14. It was an all-male operation.
15. The operation included Papa.
16. The operation included his relatives.
17. The operation included his friends.
18. They were dressed in nightshirts.
19. Their bodies glistened with perspiration.
20. They took turns cranking the crusher handle.
21. My job was to stack the crates out of the way.
22. The crates were empty.
23. The stacking was neat.

This was a prelude to what for me was the most exciting part of the evening.

24. The grapes had been mashed.
25. The empty boxes were stacked.
26. It was time for us to remove our shoes.
27. It was time for us to remove our socks.
28. It was time for us to remove our pants.
29. It was time to slip into the moisture.
30. The moisture was cool and dark.
31. This was the traditional grape stomping.
32. This was done to break up the skins.
33. I couldn't have cared less why it was necessary.
34. It was a sensual experience for me.
35. It was unlike any other experience.
36. I felt the grape residue.
37. The residue gushed between my toes.
38. I watched the new wine.
39. It turned my legs the color of Cabernet Sauvignon.
40. The color was rich and deep.

Invitation You may not have stomped grapes, but perhaps you participated in other family rituals with your father, your mother, grandparents, or siblings. Describe the details of a ritual from your family, and explain its present significance as a memory.

Appendix A
Sentence Combining
and Writing Process

This book's Introduction and unit activities have already introduced you to sentence combining (SC)—a hands-on approach for improving your sentence-making skills. The effectiveness of SC has been demonstrated in many research studies. Equally important, many thousands of students have used SC to improve their sentence fluency and to write better papers.

To transfer improved skill in sentence construction to your real writing, you need to understand how writing works. After all, writing is a *made* thing—a product of planning and scribbling and tinkering that results from what many teachers call "the writing process." While no two people follow exactly the same process, it seems clear that successful writers use a variety of productive routines. Once you understand some of these strategies and begin using the ones that make sense to you, your sentence-combining skills will take root.

This discussion of writing process has three aims. First, we'll consider the Inner Game and Outer Game of writing so that you have background for considering the processes many writers use. Then we'll examine a model of writing process to see how it might assist you with many writing tasks in school and business. Finally, we'll look at several useful strategies for generating ideas—in other words, finding something to say when you don't know what to say.

INNER GAME, OUTER GAME

Name your sport of choice—soccer, basketball, skiing, tennis, skateboarding, hockey, surfing, racquetball—whatever you enjoy. Now picture yourself on the court or playing field or riding a wave crest, in the middle of the action.

A moment's reflection will help you realize that two games occur simultaneously in any of these settings. One game is the physical action itself; the other is the psychological game that goes on inside your head. Thus, the Outer Game refers to the tennis ball zinging back and forth across the net; the Inner Game refers to the "coaching" you give yourself and to the strategies you use to keep the ball in play and score points.

Similarly, we can think of writing as an event with two simultaneous games. Right now, for example, my Outer Game is being played on an IBM PS/2 Notebook computer with a color monitor. More specifically, these words are being written on a Superbowl Sunday evening as pianist Murray Perahia plays a Mozart piano sonata. My Inner Game has been played over three days of reading, note taking, and planning. I used more Inner Game strategy tonight when I finally decided to write this material in three parts—general issues first, specific matters later.

Your Outer Game occurs whenever you transcribe your thoughts into written words. If you possess a strong set of Outer Game skills, you probably don't *think* about how to spell basic words correctly, punctuate in conventional ways, or write reasonably coherent sentences. On the other hand, if your Outer Game skills need work, SC practice can help. Why? Because SC practice improves your Outer Game *fluency*. And by helping you integrate ideas smoothly and maturely at a sentence level, SC practice "frees up" mental energy for Inner Game strategy.

I used one such Inner Game move just a few moments ago. When I found myself stuck in developing this section, I stopped and paused to reread from the heading on down. I imagined myself in your shoes—reading these words for the first time, trying to figure them out. When I reached the bottom of this section—about two paragraphs down—I realized that all of this might make more sense if I rearranged the paragraphs. So that's what I did. Then I tinkered with the wording to make the flow of thought as seamless as possible.

Another Inner Game move is occurring right now. As I write, trying to explain the interaction of Outer Game and Inner Game, I find myself pausing to wonder whether this will make any sense to you. Please understand that it's not your reading ability I doubt; rather, it's my ability to make these ideas *clear* that causes me to worry. Although I know from years of writing experience that I cannot give in to such self-doubts, I still have to coach myself to "just get the words down" so that I can work with them tomorrow. Just now, for example, I pictured my mentor, Donald Murray, who reminded me to "lower my standards."

In describing some of my planning and self-coaching, I am trying to help you understand the Inner Game of writing—at least as I understand it. I want you to see that the frustrations you feel as a writer are the same ones I feel. The truth of the matter is really quite simple: *Writing is hard work for all of us, not just for you.* The whole idea of the Inner Game is to find ways of working "smarter," not harder.

A "SHAPING UP, SHIPPING OUT" MODEL

It's possible to think of the Inner Game of writing as a series of strategic moves that flow from and into one another. Let's look at one such model of writing process to see whether it might hold interest for you. Cycle 1 outlines a process for "shaping up" a draft of writing; cycle 2 focuses on the process of working with a draft so that it can be "shipped out."

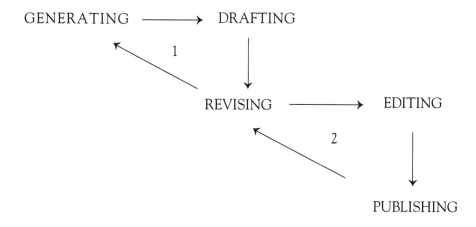

Notice the forward-pointing arrows in the model. It probably makes sense to you that *generating* ideas (say, in a list) would reasonably precede any attempt at *drafting* a paper. By the same token, *drafting* would logically precede any effort at *revising* ideas, just as *editing* would come before *publishing.*

What you may be puzzled about are arrows that point *back* toward earlier activities. For example, one arrow points from *revising* toward *generating,* and another one points from *publishing* toward *revising.* What do these "recursive" (backward-pointing) arrows suggest?

In Cycle 1 the recursive arrow indicates what most writers know from personal experience—that the process of *revising* the content of a paper or the organization of ideas often stimulates a new direction or angle for writing. In other words, the act of getting ideas down—then tinkering with them—can trigger a whole new cycle of *generating* and *drafting* activity. This recursive loop has often been compared to a process of discovery, of finding out "what you didn't know you knew."

A similar recursive loop occurs in Cycle 2—from *publishing* to *revising* to *generating.* But how can this be? Once a piece of writing is published, isn't the writer finished with it? Perhaps not. For example, this edition of *Sentence Combining* grows out of work that was published twenty years ago. The original book contained no discussion of the inner and outer games of writing; also absent was any mention of a "shaping up, shipping out" model to describe the writing process. The fact that I'm still trying to get this book right leads me to agree with the poet Paul Valery—that writing is "never finished, only abandoned."

Generating techniques include, among others, list making, clustering, sketching, reading and taking notes, asking and answering questions, free-writing, and outlining. Such writing—often in words and phrases, not sentences—is sometimes called a "zero draft," the stage before a first draft. Many writers find that talking through their ideas with others helps prepare them for *drafting.*

In *drafting* a paper, you establish an initial shape and a direction for your writing. Generally, it's a good idea to work relatively fast when developing a first draft, focusing mainly on content (what you want to say). After a first draft is finished, try setting it aside for a day or two and then coming back to it for a more critical second look. Typically, your teacher or employer never sees this draft; instead, it provides the raw material that you use for *revising.*

As the model above indicates, *revising* lies at the *heart* of the writing process. During revision, your emphasis is still on content (getting the ideas right), but organization and focus are also high priorities. Often you'll ask yourself basic questions: *What's my message? Where is this going? How can I organize more clearly?* In all likelihood, you'll rearrange paragraphs, add points of emphasis or detail, and begin to delete irrelevant or distracting material. It's usually quite helpful at this stage to have other students (or your instructor) read your draft and offer constructive response.

While *editing* may occur at any stage of the writing process, it makes most sense toward the end—when content, organization, and focus are firmly established. Editing refers to decisions about word choice and phrasing as well as to the process of "cleaning up" any errors in spelling, punctuation, and usage. It may interest you to know that *unskilled* student writers tend to be preoccupied with editing at the early stages of writing. The problem with premature editing is that it blocks the writer's attention to the larger issues of content and structure.

Publishing may take many forms. Distributing an updated résumé is a form of publishing. So is handing in a paper for a term project. So is presenting a portfolio of your best pieces of writing. Remember that you can publish your work among family and friends simply by sharing it with them. Whenever you get a response from another human being about your written words, you have published something.

How to Generate Ideas

Let's turn now from a general discussion of writing process to seven specific strategies you can use to generate ideas. These strategies are tools for thinking. Find the ones that work for you, and make them part of your writing routine.

Try practicing these approaches in connection with sentence combining. When you find a writing Invitation that appeals to you, turn to this section and use a new *generating* strategy. Over time, you'll discover the techniques that work best in your personal writing process. The aim of these activities is to help you relax and work productively.

Talking   Have you ever "unloaded" your problems on a close friend? Most of us remember such close encounters because they help us to *think through* an issue or decision. Generally, we don't ask the friend to solve our problem; after all, that's a matter of personal responsibility. We simply ask the friend to listen—to hear us out as we try to talk our way through it.

In much the same way, talking can help you solve problems in writing. As you explain your writing difficulty, your listener probably nods, smiles, grunts, and frowns; occasionally, he or she may ask questions, look puzzled, or offer suggestions. Working in this way can help you clarify *what* you want to say as well as *how* it might be said. Why? Because you've rehearsed your ideas before writing them!

Listing   Perhaps you're the type of person who makes a list before shopping or beginning an afternoon of errands. The list helps you use time well because it gets you organized. You may also have discovered how helpful a list can be in planning your study time. By budgeting your time and setting priorities, you take control of your academic life.

For many writers, too, a list serves as a memory aid, one that's quick, efficient, and easy to use. Often you can list writing ideas in a few minutes or less. Such a list is easy to rearrange by drawing arrows or by recopying; also, you can make the list more detailed by adding categories. Here, for example, is the list I used when writing this section.

Generating Strategies
- Talking to others
- Making lists
- Clustering technique
- Different kinds of sketches,
    maps, time lines, doodles
- Freewriting
- Creating questions
- Outlining

Generally speaking, listing works well when you're familiar with your material, and you simply need a way to get yourself moving. For example, when you are writing an essay exam, the simple list is a powerful tool for giving yourself a sense of direction.

Clustering   You saw above that the list is straightforward and orderly. A "cluster," on the other hand, works differently. Clustering taps visual imagery, word associations, and memory in a playful, personal way. For this reason, clustering is a strategy you'll want to try as you work with SC Invitations.

Here's a sample cluster that uses "Generating Strategies" as its nucleus:

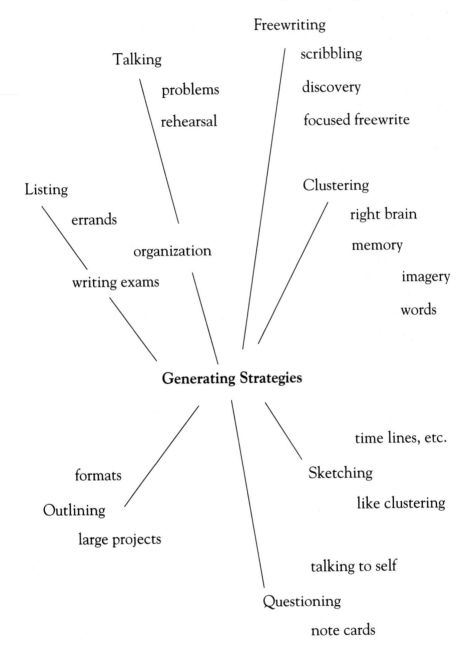

Freewriting

Talking

scribbling

problems

discovery

rehearsal

focused freewrite

Listing

Clustering

errands

right brain

organization

memory

writing exams

imagery

words

Generating Strategies

time lines, etc.

formats

Sketching

Outlining

like clustering

large projects

talking to self

Questioning

note cards

The key to clustering is allowing yourself the freedom to be creative. First of all, simply relax and put your topic in the center of a blank page. Let your mind make its associations in any way it chooses. Write down key words or phrases as they come, without excluding anything. Use lines to connect related words and ideas; have fun with the process.

Over a period of five minutes or so, watch the cluster emerge on your notepad. As it unfolds, you will sometimes feel a sudden "click" of understanding or a "flash" of insight. Once you experience this sudden sense of how to write your paper, you're ready to start drafting.

Sketching   Try making sketches as a way of generating writing ideas. For example, if you're trying to recall events from your childhood for a personal essay, you can sketch a simple map of your neighborhood or home. The process of drawing a map will stimulate many details in your mind. You can then use the sketch to talk through important memories with a writing partner. Following such a two-step process of prewriting, you'll find yourself ready to draft a strong, interesting memoir.

Another type of sketch is the time line. Let's say, for example, that you've sketched a map and talked with a writing partner as described above. Now you might use a personal time line to outline a series of events; this would help you begin writing.

September Turning Point

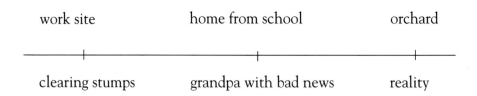

Other types of sketches include stick figures. For example, if you're reading a short story, you might sketch key figures as you understand them. The henpecked husband would be a small figure; the villain would have an evil smile or devil's horns; the wide-eyed free spirit would have hair flowing in the wind. As you get ready to write a critical analysis, these sketches will cue your memories of the story.

Another type of sketch is the diagram or model. An example of such a sketch is the two-cycle model of writing process that I used in the section "A 'Shaping Up, Shipping Out' Model." By using a sketch to outline a complex process, I tried to make the process easier to understand.

Freewriting
Try the process of nonstop freewriting when you're having trouble with a writing assignment. The aim with this technique is to get the words flowing. Don't worry about how your writing relates to the topic or assignment. Just write—thinking "aloud" on paper.

As your fingers scribble across a notepad or dance nonstop over a computer keyboard, you begin to voice your frustration and think about *why* you're stuck. The idea, remember, is to let the words flow, without any pause. What happens typically is that you begin to think *on* paper, not in your head. Words lead to sentences, which lead to ideas.

The process of nonstop freewriting sometimes triggers a release of blocked ideas. This is an exciting event, one that you will surely enjoy once you experience it. Many writers then use *focused freewriting* as a second step to drafting. Choose a word, phrase, or idea from the first writing as a springboard for the second. Before you know it, you have material that you'll be able to incorporate into your paper.

Questioning
Sometimes, because we're so focused on the problems of writing, we overlook the obvious: What are the reader's *questions* about my topic? Making a list of questions from the reader's viewpoint provides a fresh way to approach the challenge of writing. Also, once you have a list of questions, you can begin to work on organizing your paper effectively.

One strategy you might try for longer projects is to put questions on note cards. These cards can serve as organizers for your library research, face-to-face interviews, or other methods of gathering information. Of course, questions can easily be converted into topic sentences that lead into paragraphs. Also, you might try leaving a question or two as section headings or paragraph openers. While the device of the rhetorical question can become tired if you overuse it, don't hesitate to give it a try. It often works extremely well.

The key point about questions is that they serve as intellectual tools. Once you have questions in mind, your background reading and your writing have purpose. In other words, questions not only help your writing but also give focus to your thinking.

Outlining Many teachers and students think of outlining as old-fashioned, and in a way it is. However, when you're faced with a research paper, proposal, or report, you may want to use an outlining strategy of some kind. You'll prepare an outline for basically the same reason that you carry a road map when traveling cross-country: you don't want to get lost somewhere along the way. Also, once you have a plan to work from, you can concentrate on *what* you're saying, not whether it's organized.

Of course, a good outline is not a straitjacket. In the process of drafting and developing your paper, you may have new insights that you want to incorporate. That's to be expected, not avoided. As noted above, an outline is like a road map. If you want to take some side roads along the journey, you can use the outline to find your way back to the main highway.

The note-card technique described under "Questioning" above can help you develop a topic outline. Simply put key words or phrases on separate note cards; then spread the cards out on a large surface, and sort them into categories. Deal with the categories one by one, arranging the cards into sequences. Finally, transfer your working plan from the note cards into some sort of outline.

Here's a topic outline for the material on outlining:

> **Outlining**
>   A. Old-fashioned but useful for long documents
>   B. Similar to a road map; not a straitjacket
>   C. Note-card technique to develop an outline
>   1. Use key words and phrases—separate cards
>   2. Put in categories—then sequence
>   3. Create an outline from cards

And here's a simple "semantic web"—a different sort of outline that expresses the same ideas as the one above:

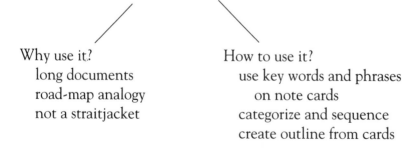

Outlining

Why use it?
  long documents
  road-map analogy
  not a straitjacket

How to use it?
  use key words and phrases
    on note cards
  categorize and sequence
  create outline from cards

Appendix B
Sentence and
Paragraph Strategies

Perhaps you've tried some SC exercises, and you're now ready for some advice on sentence and paragraph strategies. If so, this is the material you've been looking for. You can find additional minilessons on specific grammar and punctuation topics in a companion book—*A Writer's Toolbox* (forthcoming from McGraw-Hill).

In this section we'll consider five minilessons of writing strategy. Here's the sequence:

Parallelism in Sentences

Variety in Sentences

Choosing Effective Sentences

Paragraph Organization

Paragraph Packaging

These lessons provide introductions to important writing topics. If you'd like additional information, check with your instructor, who can refer you to other materials or provide further in-class examples to answer your questions.

PARALLELISM IN SENTENCES

Parallel lines run side by side—like a railroad track. This same idea can be applied to sentences. With parallel (or balanced) construction, you use repeated phrases or sentence patterns. As long as you repeat the pattern, you don't "derail" your reader.

Shown below in boldface type is an example of balanced prepositional phrases:

> Senior citizens are up at the crack of dawn.
>
> Senior citizens are without other places to go.
>
> Senior citizens head for their local hangout.

> **Up at the crack of dawn** and **without other places to go,** senior citizens head for their local hangout.

Let's add an appositive phrase to the sentence above, one that describes the local hangout:

> Senior citizens—**up at the crack of dawn, without other places to go**—head for their local hangout, **a fast-food restaurant.**

Here you see parallel noun phrases—*their local hangout* and *a fast-food restaurant.*

Of course, parallelism can involve more than a pair of phrases or sentences. Shown below are two examples in which noun phrases occur in a series.

> The men come dressed in a standard uniform—**baseball cap, nylon windbreaker, checkered pants,** and **running shoes.**
>
> OR
>
> The widows wear **knit sweaters, blue or pink polyester pants,** and **sturdy, old-fashioned shoes.**

Remember, any sort of series that repeats a grammatical element is called a "balanced" structure—or "parallelism" for short.

Let's now look at another example of parallelism, this time in verb phrases with verb forms called "participles."

> They arrive rain or shine.
>
> They look for a newspaper.
>
> They look for a cup of coffee.
>
> They hope for a friendly smile

> They arrive rain or shine, **looking for a newspaper and a cup of coffee** and **hoping for a friendly smile.**

The parallel verb phrases begin with *looking* and *hoping*. Nested within the first phrase is more parallelism (*a newspaper* and *a cup of coffee*). These latter two phrases are once again noun phrases.

So far, we've considered simple examples of balanced (or parallel) structure. As you might guess, parallelism can get more interesting and complicated. Shown below is a sentence with two main clauses balanced against each other; within each clause are parallel phrases.

> Some seniors are physically sound.
>
> They are mentally alert.
>
> They are happily adjusted to retirement.
>
> Other seniors are financially strapped.
>
> They are emotionally starved.

> Some seniors are **physically sound, mentally alert**, and **happily adjusted to retirement;** others, however, are **financially strapped** and **emotionally starved.**

In this example, you see parallelism both at the clause level and at the level of repeated phrases (in boldface).

What about problems with parallelism? One common problem results from trying to use two different types of phrases—say a noun phrase and a verb phrase—in parallel fashion. Here's an example of such a *problem* sentence (marked with an asterisk):

> *****Discussions about old age** and **sharing a cup of coffee** help seniors cope with their loneliness.

To fix this sentence, either make both of the boldfaced items noun phrases or make both of them verb phrases:

> **Discussions about old age** and **a shared cup of coffee** help seniors cope with their loneliness.
>
> OR
>
> Seniors cope with their loneliness by **discussing old age** and **sharing a cup of coffee.**

Both sentences above solve the problem. The first uses noun phrases, while the second uses verb phrases.

Parallelism problems can occur when you're in a hurry—or when you haven't proofread carefully. Let's see if you can spot what's wrong with the sentence below and determine how it might be fixed.

> *The seniors may vary **in age, how much income,** and **what race they are,** yet their social needs are similar.

The problem results from three different types of phrases being used together. To fix this sentence, why not try this?

> The seniors may vary **in age, in income,** and **in race,** yet their social needs are similar.
>   OR
> Although their **ages, incomes,** and **races** may vary, their social needs are similar.

Thus, the secret of good parallel structure is to set up a pattern, stick with it, and read your words aloud. Now that you understand parallelism, read the section "Variety in Sentences."

VARIETY IN SENTENCES

What is it they say about variety? That it adds "spice" to life? That "different is good"? What's true for life (and fast food) is no less true for sentences. Variety *matters*, not just for its own sake but for the emphasis it adds to ideas.

To explore sentence variety, let's work with the next cluster of sentences. While these sentences won't lead to any literary masterpiece, we can have fun using them to learn.

> Alice seemed callous.
>
> She was at home in her palace.
>
> Her palace was near Dallas.
>
> She lived without malice.

As you combine this cluster, you may use *but* to create a "balanced" sentence, one with two halves:

> Alice seemed callous in her Dallas palace, **but** she lived without malice.

Or you may use *although* to make the first half of the sentence depend on the second half:

> **Although** Alice seemed callous in her Dallas palace, she lived without malice.

Or you may reverse the wording of the first half and make the second half almost separate from the first:

> In her Dallas palace, Alice seemed callous; **however**, she lived without malice.

Or you may disregard connectors altogether and use a different approach to combining:

> **Seemingly callous** in her Dallas palace, Alice lived without malice.

As you whisper the four sentences above, what you probably notice is their *variety*—in structure and rhythm. In a way, each sentence has a unique "voice." Each conveys basically the same message, but it does so in its own way. This, in a nutshell, is what we mean by sentence variety.

Beneath the surface of any written sentences are many others, just waiting to be discovered and considered. It's you who makes the decisions about which sentences to keep and which to reject. To do this, you read the *context* of surrounding sentences, listening to the flow of meaning. Then, trusting your instincts, you begin to rearrange, to add, and to trim back where necessary.

Let's say, for example, that you wanted the "Alice" sentences to emphasize her appearance of callousness, not her lack of malice. To accomplish this, you'd work with structure once again, putting the key idea in the main sentence.

> Alice, who lived without malice in a Dallas palace, seemed callous.
> > OR
>
> Living in a Dallas palace without malice, Alice seemed callous.
> > OR
>
> A Dallas palace is where Alice lived without malice; nevertheless, she seemed callous.
> > OR
>
> Although Alice's life in a Dallas palace was without malice, she seemed callous.

Notice again: Each sentence "says" the same thing as the others, but each does so in a unique way. Notice, too, that the sentences all have different opening words.

Looking at opening words in your own writing will help you determine whether you have reasonable sentence variety. Of course, if all sentences begin with the same words—or almost the same ones—it's a safe bet that you can revise with an eye (and ear) toward varied sentences. The goal, always, is communication that engages your reader and handles your subject effectively; sentence variety is simply a tool to accomplish that goal.

How else can sentence variety be achieved? You can experiment with punctuation, such as a pair of dashes:

> Alice seemed callous—at home in her Dallas palace—yet she lived without malice.

Or you can reverse the regular word order, again using punctuation:

> At home, in her Dallas palace, lived Alice—seemingly callous, but without malice.

Or you can try *it* as a sentence opener:

> It was without malice, in her Dallas palace, that seemingly callous Alice lived.

Or you can see what happens with *what*:

> What seemed callous, despite her absence of malice, was Alice's life in a Dallas palace.

Or you can combine sentences as simply as possible:

> Seemingly callous, Alice lived without malice in her Dallas palace.

The last sentence above—the short one—deserves further comment. As you explore options through sentence combining, you may conclude that "long is good" and "short is bad." Nothing could be further from the truth. Why? Because *short* sentences are probably your most powerful tool for achieving variety!

Variety in sentences comes naturally as you try new structures, read with care, and—above all—listen to what you have written. Read "Choosing Effective Sentences" for more on variety.

CHOOSING EFFECTIVE SENTENCES

How do you know which sentences to choose? To answer that question, let's combine clusters, make some choices, and see the results in paragraph form. Our tongue-in-cheek topic? "Surviving School"! Study the X and Y sentences below for each cluster.

1.1 Gaining an extension is not easy.
1.2 The extension is for a term paper.
1.3 A formula works for some students.
1.4 The formula is time-tested.

1X
Gaining an extension is not easy for a term paper, but a time-tested formula works for some students.

1Y
Although gaining an extension for a term paper is not easy, a time-tested formula works for some students.

Sentence 1X, as written, is confusing and ungrammatical. By contrast, 1Y is much clearer and easier to follow.

2.1 The student's approach should be shuffling.
2.2 The student's approach should be deferential.
2.3 The approach is to the instructor.
2.4 It should not be arrogant.
2.5 It should not be demanding.

2X
The student's approach to the instructor should be shuffling and deferential, not arrogant or demanding.

2Y
The approach of the student to the instructor should not be so much arrogant or demanding as shuffling and deferential.

Sentence 2X is five words shorter and easier to read than 2Y. Therefore, 2X is the better choice.

3.1 The aim is to signal humility.
3.2 The aim is to signal sincerity.
3.3 The aim is to signal respect.
3.4 The respect is profound.

3X
The aim is to signal not only humility and sincerity but also profound respect.

3Y
To signal humility, sincerity, and profound respect—that is the aim.

In the context of previous choices, sentences 3X and 3Y seem to offer a toss-up. Which would you choose? Perhaps another sentence?

4.1 The student should apologize.
4.2 The apology is for the interruption.
4.3 The student should say this.
4.4 "The class is a great learning experience."

4X
After apologizing for the interruption, the student should say, "The class is a great learning experience."

4Y
Before saying that the class is "a great learning experience," the student should apologize for the interruption.

Sentence 4X is stronger because it delays the most important words to the end (where they belong). Also, the sequence of events in 4X seems clearer than in 4Y.

5.1 A moment's hesitation adds drama.
5.2 A furrowed brow adds intensity.
5.3 They suggest inner turmoil.

5X
As a way of suggesting an inner turmoil, a moment's hesitation and a furrowed brow add both drama and intensity.

5Y
A moment's hesitation and a furrowed brow add dramatic intensity by suggesting inner turmoil.

Sentence 5Y seems more effective than 5X. First, its pattern contrasts with that of the previous choice (4X). Second, 5Y is six words shorter—and easier to read—than 5X.

6.1 The student may now allude to the paper.
6.2 The paper is a quest.

6.3   The quest is fascinating and challenging.
6.4   The quest requires "just a little more time."

6X	6Y
The student may now allude to the paper as a fascinating and challenging quest—one that requires "just a little more time."	An allusion to the paper as a quest which is fascinating and challenging but which requires "just a little more time" may now be made by the student.

In context, sentence 6X is stronger, clearer, and shorter than 6Y; its dash and appositive are quite effective. Sentence 6Y, with its passive voice and wordiness, seems bloated by comparison.

Now that we've combined sentences and made our choices, let's see what the results look like in paragraph form:

(1) Although gaining an extension for a term paper is not easy, a time-tested formula works for some students. (2) The student's approach to the instructor should be shuffling and deferential, not arrogant or demanding. (3) The aim is to signal humility, sincerity, and profound respect. (4) After apologizing for the interruption, the student should say, "The class is a great learning experience." (5) A moment's hesitation and a furrowed brow add dramatic intensity by suggesting inner turmoil. (6) The student may now allude to the paper as a fascinating and challenging quest—one that requires "just a little more time."

PARAGRAPH ORGANIZATION

In the introduction to Unit 3, you learned about paragraphs as "clusters" or "packages" of sentences. Let's now explore further how some paragraphs are organized. While these points won't cover all situations, they may help you to think about the paragraphs in your own writing, particularly those that explain or persuade.

Most paragraphs in your school writing have a main point, or *topic*. On a midterm exam, for example, you might write about DNA molecules, the law of supply and demand, or the causes of child abuse. Each of these topics can be approached in different ways, but a time-proven method is to begin with a *topic sentence*. Such a sentence is usually a generalization that points the direction for sentences that follow.

Suppose that you want to compare two short stories. To do so, you might begin with a topic sentence like this:

> In my opinion, "Nighthawk" is superior to "Summer Wind" for three reasons.

Notice how such a topic sentence sets up what follows. It tells the reader what stories are being compared, which of the stories is (in the writer's opinion) more effective, and how many reasons will be discussed. Such an approach is clear and businesslike. It gets the job done.

Of course, setting direction is one thing, but the next task is to develop the *supporting details* for the topic sentence. Do the next sentences fill the bill by providing reasons?

> First, "Nighthawk" has fully developed, interesting characters rather than the stereotypes we find in "Summer Wind."
>
> Second, the plot of "Nighthawk" creates a world that involves the reader, whereas "Summer Wind" is boringly predictable.
>
> Third, the narrator of "Nighthawk" challenges us to think about real ideas, not the soap opera themes of "Summer Wind."

Such sentences develop the generalization in the topic sentence by offering a viewpoint on characterization, plot, and theme. Notice also that each supporting detail is tied to the topic sentence by the transition words *first, second,* and *third.*

Now suppose that the emerging paragraph concludes this way:

> In what follows, I will amplify each of these points.

Suddenly our paragraph becomes an *introduction* to a more extended discussion. As readers, we can anticipate that we'll probably read three more "chunks" of text, each focused on a key point from the introductory paragraph. In that essay, it's logical that each point above will become the gist of a *new* topic sentence and that the writer will marshal evidence from the two stories to back up the assertions. Thus, this paragraph *organizes* the essay.

Here's what we've learned so far:

> Paragraphs often have topic sentences followed by supporting details; a paragraph can stand by itself but also serve other functions in an essay; and the details in one paragraph can become the topic sentences in subsequent paragraphs.

(Notice, incidentally, that *this* paragraph provides a summary and makes a transition to a new topic in this minilesson.)

Of course, not all paragraphs are as highly structured as the one comparing two short stories. In fact, most aren't. Moreover, not all paragraphs have a "top-down" organization, with the topic sentence coming first. For example, compare the following patterns of organization. Can you imagine how each might be effective?

General-to-Specific
It is clear that the island
    needs a change in leadership.

Unemployment is rising.

Inflation is at record levels.

The tax structure is unjust.

Enemies threaten security.

Specific-to-General
Unemployment is rising.

Inflation is at record levels.

The tax structure is unjust.

Enemies threaten security.

It is clear that the island
    needs a change in leader-
    ship.

The left paragraph begins with a topic sentence, which is followed by supporting details. Conversely, the right paragraph has the topic sentence "emerge" from its list of reasons. Both paragraphs are organized, but they work in very different ways.

Most of your paragraphs will probably have the topic sentence *up front*. This strategy is effective when you're defining terms, explaining principles, and providing examples. But arguments may have more punch when the topic sentence comes *last*. In the next paragraph you see this principle of organization demonstrated.

Some people argue that colleges should not require freshmen to take a course in writing.

But, unfortunately, many students have real difficulties with written expression.

Eliminating such a requirement might be reasonable under other conditions.

If students were better trained in writing before college, or if college faculty would teach writing as part of their courses, freshmen writing would probably be unnecessary.

Clearly, however, the conditions described above do not exist at most schools.

Therefore, writing continues to be a reasonable requirement for most college freshmen.

As you can see, your *purposes* as a writer help you decide where to put your topic sentence. When purposes are clear, such decisions often take care of themselves.

PARAGRAPH PACKAGING

Recall from Unit 3 the discussion of paragraph packaging—the idea that paragraphs are groups of related sentences "packaged" together. The packaging is basically invisible, of course—just white space at the beginning of a paragraph and more at the end. In block-style paragraphing—often found in business letters—each paragraph is surrounded by white space but not indented.

To understand how sentences are packaged into paragraphs, let's work with ten sentences to see where they might logically be divided into two packages (or chunks) of meaning. First read the sentences; then ask yourself where they should be separated.

1. Some people, when faced with a writing problem, apply the "brute force" method.
2. They continue doing the same thing—only harder.
3. As they fume and fuss, scratching out what they have just written, they make countless false starts.
4. All this rewriting increases their mental and physical tension, which further blocks their writing.
5. Ironically, the harder they try, the worse things become.
6. Other people, when faced with similar blocks in their writing, take a more productive approach.
7. When things are not going well, they completely *change* what they are doing for a short period.
8. They sip a soft drink, get some exercise, or take care of an errand to use different muscles and energies.
9. This "sidestep" method releases tension and permits the subconscious mind to work on the problem.
10. Then they return to their writing with increased zest and creativity.

It's possible, of course, to leave the sentences as they are, without *any* paragraph break. But most people, when studying these sentences, say that a "natural" break occurs between sentences 5 and 6. They visualize two paragraphs—the first with sentences 1 to 5, the second with sentences 6 to 10. The first deals with a writing approach that often doesn't work, the second with one that works for some people. This seems like a logical division.

Let's suppose you now want to repackage the two paragraphs into *four* chunks of meaning—for a newspaper article, say. Since most newspapers have very brief paragraphs because of their narrow columns, such a task is not unusual. Take a few moments now to reread the sentences above. Where would you subdivide?

This division task is harder than the first one, and you may find disagreement in your class about the "right" answer. However, many people repackage the ten sentences into four paragraphs like this: 1 to 3, 4 and 5, 6 to 8, and 9 and 10. Of course, such short paragraphs are not typical of most writing that you do in school or in the business world. The point here is to help you understand what paragraphs are—a means of grouping (or packaging) sentences.

Let's now consider a different kind of packaging problem—the sentence that doesn't belong in a paragraph. This is a very common writing difficulty, even when writers have good ideas. Read the next sentences, and pick out the one sentence that should *not* be included here:

1. Getting into a productive frame of mind is a problem for many beginning writers.
2. The typical approach is to wait for "inspiration."
3. An alternative solution is to find a comfortable spot for writing, to come to this place regularly, and to set realistic goals for each work period.
4. Most beginners find that "inspiration" takes care of itself when these conditions are met.
5. Revision is another problem when one is learning to write.

Notice above that the first four sentences share the same topic—a *productive frame of mind*. With sentence 5 comes a switch in topic. Therefore, sentence 5 does not belong in this paragraph.

Here's a final paragraph with an out-of-place sentence. Read the sentences carefully, hunting for the one that doesn't belong.

1. Revision is another problem when one is learning to write.
2. Beginners often rely on a single draft, not realizing that good prose almost always requires revision.
3. Professionals, on the other hand, continually reread and revise, searching for better ways to express meanings.

4. Beginners often have trouble getting started, whereas professionals have regular writing habits and routines.

5. Differences in the quality (and amount) of revision usually stem from differences in attitude.

6. An uncaring attitude usually results in a single draft, but a caring attitude produces revisions of high quality.

The topic of the paragraph, expressed in sentence 1, is *revision*. Notice that all sentences except the fourth one deal with revision. Although sentence 4 (like sentences 2 and 3) contrasts beginners and professionals, it doesn't deal with the topic of revision. Therefore, it doesn't belong in the paragraph.

You can learn a great deal about paragraph packaging simply by observing what good writers *do*—in newspaper articles, magazines, and books. Learn from the professionals. They won't steer you wrong.

Credits

Baker, Russell. Reprinted from GROWING UP by Russell Baker, © 1982. Used with permission of Congdon & Weed, Inc., Chicago.

Buscaglia, Leo, From the PAPA, MY FATHER: A CELEBRATION OF DADS by Leo Buscaglia. Copyright © 1989 by Leo F. Buscaglia, Inc. Reprinted by permission.

Crow Dog, Mary. From the book LAKOTA WOMAN by Mary Crow Dog, Copyright © 1990 by Mary Crow Dog & Richard Erdoes. Used with the permission of Grove/Atlantic Monthly Press. To order call 800-937-5557.

Excerpt adapted from pages 160-161 from AN AMERICAN CHILDHOOD by Annie Dillard. Copyright © 1987 by Annie Dillard. Reprinted by permission of HarperCollins Publishers, Inc.

Ishikawa, Yoshimi, From STRAWBERRY ROAD by Yoshimi Ishikawa, translated by Eve Zimmerman, published by Kodansha International Ltd. Copyright © 1991 by Yoshimi Ishikawa. Reprinted by permission. All rights reserved.

Keller, Helen, THE STORY OF MY LIFE. Garden City: Doubleday & Company, Inc., 1954.

Kingston, Maxine Hong. From THE WOMAN WARRIOR by Maxine Hong Kingston. Copyright © 1975, 1976 by Maxine Hong Kingston. Reprinted by permission of Alfred A. Knopf, Inc.

L'Engle, Madeleine. Excerpt from TWO-PART INVENTION by Madeleine L'Engle. Copyright © 1988 by Crosswicks Ltd. Reprinted by permission of Farrar, Straus & Giroux, Inc.

Maclean, Norman. From "A River Runs Through It" in A RIVER RUNS THROUGH IT AND OTHER STORIES by Norman Maclean. Copyright © 1976 by The University of Chicago. Reprinted by permission.

Meltzer, Milton. From STARTING FROM HOME by Milton Meltzer. Copyright © 1988 by Milton Meltzer. Used by permission of Viking Penguin, a division of Penguin Books USA Inc.

Moon, William Least Heat, BLUE HIGHWAYS: A JOURNEY INTO AMERICA. Boston: Little, Brown and Company, 1982, p. 181.

Soto, Gary. Reprinted from "The Catfish" in A SUMMER LIFE by Gary Soto. © 1990 by University Press of New England. By permission of University Press of New England.

Tan, Amy. Reprinted by permission of The Putnam Publishing Group from THE JOY LUCK CLUB by Amy Tan. Copyright © 1989 by Amy Tan.

Thomas, Lewis, ET CETERA, ET CETERA: NOTES OF A WORD-WATCHER. Boston: Little, Brown and Company, 1990, pp. 93-94.

Uchida, Yoshiko. From DESERT EXILE by Yoshiko Uchida. Copyright © 1982 by Yoshiko Uchida. Reprinted by permission of University of Washington Press.